Broken Frame

Also by New Academia Publishing

TURKEY'S MODERNIZATION
Refugees from Nazism and Atatürk's Vision, by Arnold Reisman

NATIONALISM, HISTORIOGRAPHY, AND THE (RE)CONSTRUCTION OF THE PAST, Claire Norton, ed.

ASPECTS OF BALKAN CULTURE: Social, Political, and Literary Perceptions
by Jelena Milojković-Djurić

DOOMED TO REPEAT? Terrorism and the Lessons of History, Edited by
Sean Brawley

NEW PERSPECTIVES ON SOVIETIZATION IN CENTRAL AND EASTERN EUROPE AFTER WORLD WAR II, Balázs Apor, Péter Apor and E. A. Rees, eds.

GOD, GREED, AND GENOCIDE: The Holocaust through the Centuries
by Arthur Grenke

ON THE ROAD TO BAGHDAD, or TRAVELING BICULTURALISM
Theorizing a Bicultural Approach to Contemporary World Fiction
Gönül Pultar, ed.

BROTHERS IN EXILE: A Novel of the Lives and Loves of Thomas
and Heinrich Mann, by Selig Kainer

FROM WARSAW TO WHEREVER
by Zygmunt Nagorski

JOURNEYS THROUGH VANISHING WORLDS, by Abraham Brumberg

www.newacademia.com

Broken Frame
Memoirs of a Turkish Immigrant

Fuat M. Andic

Washington, DC

Copyright © 2009 by Fuat M. Andic

New Academia Publishing, 2009

All rights reserved. No part of this book may be reproduced or transmitted in any form or by any means, electronic or mechanical, including photocopying, recording, or by any information storage and retrieval system.

Printed in the United States of America

Library of Congress Control Number: 2009936517
ISBN 978-0-9823867-6-7 paperback (alk. paper)

 An imprint of new Academia Publishing
P.O. Box 27420, Washington, DC 20038-7420

 www.newacademia.com
info@newacademia.com

Contents

Prologue   vii

1. The Beginning of the End   1
2. Roots   9
3. Born in Instanbul   31
4. Childhood Memories   53

Photo Gallery   71

5. The War Years   77
6. My Military Service   83
7. In the West   93
8. From Professor to Consultant   117

Epilogue   133

Prologue

I am a descendant of two Balkan families who, because of circumstances beyond their control, were forced to leave their native cities where their ancestors had lived for hundreds of years, thus becoming refugees. Both families adopted the same new city, Istanbul, and tried to adapt to their new surroundings and circumstances as best they could. It was a very painful experience. The memories of their lives in their native cities lingered in their minds and never faded from their hearts. I was born in Istanbul and I, too, left my city—but not because of circumstances beyond my control. Quite the contrary. I left voluntarily and opted to live in the United States.

I think an immigrant always has a dual personality. At least I do. I have been very meticulous in keeping my identity as a Turk. With Turkey's culture, history, music, and literature woven into my very marrow, I belong to the country where I was raised and the city I will always love. But since the United States is my adopted country, I am also an American. For better or for worse, I have tied my fate with its fate. Its problems are my problems; its joy, my joy.

My dual personality manifests itself in various ways. Here in the United States, with my inalienable right, I can freely criticize the attitude my adopted country takes toward various issues whenever I deem it appropriate. I criticize the foreign policy, I criticize the educational policy, and I criticize junk food. But whenever I visit my native country, Turkey, I become very defensive if someone criticizes the United States, especially when criticism borders on disparaging comments. My counter-arguments follow one another and many times I become belligerent. Similarly, I become angry when harsh words, whether justified or not, are spoken against

Turkey in the United States. And yet in Turkey I am perhaps the severest critic. Could it be love for both? I know not.

To forget one's native land is an absolute impossibility. Memories linger; from time to time, nostalgic remembrances become companions of everyday thoughts. Although one acquires the habits and mores of one's adopted country, the old self is always there. Antagonisms and cultural clashes continue, I must admit, but they sculpt a new identity that borrows from the two cultures. I have become an American. Rationally, I love America; emotionally, I am bound to remain a Turk. I am not unhappy with my dual personality.

From time to time, I yearn to return to my city of origin. I miss Istanbul, the city I left behind. Whenever I visit, I retrace my steps of yesteryears. I visit the area and the street where once stood the tiny house in which I lived and the small square with the old oak tree in its center and benches around its trunk. I visit the cobblestone street where the grade school that I attended stood. The building is no longer there, but I can still hear the voices of the teachers and the joyful noises the children made when playing. I visit my university and can look at it only from a distance; the new security rules forbid me from entering, as they allow only staff and students. I love to smell the cool musty air of the covered bazaar. Walking through the passage that snakes from the university plaza to the entrance of the covered bazaar where the used book shops are located is an absolute necessity for me. Sometimes, just for pleasure, I even buy a book or two that I already have, recalling the bittersweet memory that I could not even afford to buy one when I was a young university student.

I cannot possibly miss a boat trip on the Bosporus. The cool breeze from the north, the blue waters that separate Asia from Europe, the tooting of the ferry that announces its arrival or departure from the stations that dot both sides of the straits—these sights and sounds evoke thousands of memories. But all of that is nothing more than a futile endeavor to relive the past. And invariably, when the time comes to return to my adopted country, I am the happiest person at the airport.

This book is not a typical autobiography. It does not tell my story in a linear fashion. Those who wish to secure a place in history write that kind of autobiography. I have no such pretension. I have written it because essentially I love to write. Another author, whose name escapes me, wrote that "Those who write their memoirs should have three characteristics: they should have something to tell, should know how to tell, and should love to tell." I know I have one of these characteristics. I love to tell. Of the second characteristic, I am not sure. Whether I have the first is for the reader to decide.

I have always loved to write, and not just books on economics. Writing even very mundane technical reports in my own field has always been pleasurable for me. At an early age I developed a special love for words, words in all the languages I know: English, French, Spanish, and most certainly Turkish. A short poem I wrote in 1979 in Spanish poses the imaginary question as to why I write. Here is the answer:

> Neither for the reader do I write
> nor for myself,
> nor to be in the pages of an anthology with a line or two
> nor even for God.
> For words I write,
> just to hear their pure sounds,
> just to see their hidden colors.
> I write just to kiss them
> to caress them
> to make love to them.
> For words I write,
> only for words.

For me, words are not strings of letters; they have internal beauty, they have souls.

I also want to write about my grandparents, whose stories have been told to me time and again, stories that will live with me forever. This book is their story as well as mine, for it also relates my experiences as I grew up, episodes that are like snapshots buried in my memory and have left deep and unforgettable impressions on me. I also recount fragments of my professional life in my adopted country.

My life combines two worlds that are thousands of miles apart from each other, physically as well as culturally. I like to think that I have combined them harmoniously, at least in my mind and in my spirit.

1
The Beginning of the End

I

It was in March 1976 that I received a phone call from my nephew informing me that my aunt had died. She was only two years older than my mother and now, after the untimely death of my mother almost twenty years earlier, she had also met her maker. She loved me very much and, after the death of my mother, became a second mother to me. She was a spinster, never married, no children; I was a surrogate son to her. It was the middle of the semester so I could not attend the funeral. Even if I had been able to go, it would have been too late. It took two days for me to travel to Istanbul from Puerto Rico, where I was teaching at the university. As my nephew had informed me, the burial was to take place the very next day. I waited impatiently until the end of the semester and flew to Istanbul on the first available flight. It was a sad homecoming to my beloved city.

The next day, I visited the cemetery, and then the office of a lawyer. I was the next of kin and she had bequeathed a sizeable inheritance to me. According to Article 498 of the Civil Code, I was the sole heir. I gave the power of attorney to the lawyer who assured me that it was an open and shut case, and within a month or two he would conclude all the formalities, at which time I would inherit what my aunt had left.

Despite the fact that she was just a grade school teacher like my mother, she had a reasonable sum that she had saved and deposited in the bank; she also owned an apartment in a nice building.

I left the lawyer's office sad but with some positive outlook, and a few days later returned to my home in San Juan. What happened thereafter is an unbelievable tragic-comic series of incidents that, had I not experienced them firsthand, I would not have believed was possible.

At first, the letters I received from the lawyer were rather encouraging. He had petitioned that I was the sole heir, and the procedure was that the judge would rule, naturally, in my favor in a single session. Then a snag developed. Information received from the Registrar of Births and Deaths showed that my grandmother was still alive; therefore, she was the legal heir. I was totally bewildered. She had died in 1947 at the ripe old age of seventy-five. If she were alive she would have been one hundred and plus years old—a ridiculous impossibility. Those who knew her and could attest to the fact that she was dead were also dead.

These facts apparently did not move the judge. Legally, without two reliable witnesses, he could not rule that she was, in fact, deceased. The lawyer asked me to supply the names of possible witnesses. I had none. Her doctor was dead. Our neighbors in our old neighborhood, Sultantepe, who knew my grandmother, were either dead or had moved and I had lost contact with them. My answer did not discourage the lawyer; he responded that he could find some people in our old neighborhood who would swear on their honor that she was indeed dead and they had witnessed her passing away. It would not cost very much, as he had a list of professional false witnesses with modest fees. The whole enterprise would not take more than a couple of months. Just a bit more patience was required.

I waited for three months for the next letter from my lawyer. That letter was not very encouraging. Yes, my grandmother, thanks to false witnesses, was now legally dead and buried, but my mother appeared to be alive and well and, therefore, she was the legal heir.

I could not believe my eyes. My mother had died in 1956 after a long illness and it was so registered in the records of the Registrar. At least so I had thought. Obviously I was wrong. Now I had to relive the pain of losing her while pacing in the musty corridors of the courthouse among the faceless crowd. The lawyer again wanted

The Beginning of the End

the name of two witnesses, since it was necessary to appeal to the court, produce two witnesses, and eliminate my mother once more. It should not take long, the lawyer wrote, at most three months. Thank God, no false witnesses were necessary, since some family members who had witnessed my mother's very last minutes were quite willing to appear before the judge.

It took longer than the lawyer had expected, but finally he called me and informed me that it was all settled. All I had to do was to go to Istanbul, sign some papers—just routine, he said—and the inheritance would be mine. As soon as the semester was over at the university, I was again in Istanbul. I went to see the lawyer where, lo and behold, another surprise was waiting for me.

"Are you aware that your aunt was married?" asked the lawyer. My aunt was never married, never even had a male friend. In fact, there were rumors that she did not like men. It was hush-hush of course, family honor and all that, but I knew full well that she had never been married, most assuredly.

This innovative lawyer was not going to be deterred with a minor setback, as he put it. There were ways and means to remedy the situation. What he told me was quite Kafkaesque. He would, with some hefty sums, get the Registrar's office to work in an entry that, yes, she was married, but her husband had died before her, or they were divorced some years back.

I could not believe my ears, yet the lawyer was completely serious. It could be done. "Money," he said, "there is nothing that money cannot solve." The only thing was that it would take some ingenuity and some time.

I did not ask him how long it would take; I did not ask him how he would do it. All I wanted to do was to get the hell out of his office as fast as possible just to keep my sanity. "Do whatever is necessary," I said, and left.

I entered the first coffee house I saw and ordered a Turkish coffee without sugar. Into what kind of justice system had Turkey sunk? How could a person already dead need to have a judge's decision to be really dead? How could a non-existing husband be declared legally dead, or divorced? How?

Dozens of scenarios began to buzz in my head. I imagined a room, the court room; my lawyer and two witnesses are there, as well as the judge—a plump, middle-aged, bald, bespectacled man listening to the witness who has just sworn, on his honor, to tell the truth, nothing but the truth.

"Your honor, we were then living in Sultantepe *(lie)*; I was in the fifth grade. One day my mother told me that my teacher's mother had died and I was to attend the funeral procession *(lie)*. It must have been some thirty years back, your honor."

The other witness, looking very pious with a long white beard, sounds even more convincing. "Your honor, some thirty years ago I was a *müezzin*, a prayer caller, in Sultantepe *(lie)*. I was told that Aisha Hanım had died. She was a much respected, much esteemed old lady in our neighborhood. I immediately went to her house *(lie)*. I remember her daughter, who was a teacher in the neighborhood grade school, and her grandson were crying *(lie)*. I performed the last rites *(lies, lies, lies)* and I also joined the funeral procession *(lie)*. That is the God's truth, your honor *(the biggest lie)*."

The judge knows that they are lies and yet, following the due process of law, he was officially killing my grandmother for the second time and adjourning the court.

The more I imagined the court sessions, the sicker I felt. I was nauseated and had a splitting headache. Leaving the coffee house, I walked aimlessly for a while. I noticed the streets were empty; no cars passed me by. I didn't pay any attention to shop windows, just gazed at emptiness. Finally I decided to go to the Covered Bazaar, perhaps just to spend money, to buy something, anything, certainly nothing that I needed. After entering the bazaar, the cool air helped me feel a bit better.

Almost involuntarily, I walked toward the alley where all the antique shops conglomerated. Perhaps I would buy an antique ring for my wife, or maybe a brooch. She already had so many pieces, but I said to myself, "One more won't make any difference, and she might like it." Besides, I knew that it would make me feel good. Whenever I am angry, buying something unnecessary, something utterly useless, or something superfluous gives me some comfort, some relief. I know it has no logic, it has no reason or rhyme; I guess it just distracts me, be it momentarily.

I entered two different shops and looked around, but I didn't care for the items the shopkeepers showed me. Either they were unattractive or the prices were way out of line. The third shop I entered seemed much better. There were some antique brooches at reasonable prices. I selected one and, as custom dictates, began to bargain with the shopkeeper. In Turkey, one does not buy an antique at the first price cited. In fact, not to bargain is considered an insult to the seller. The price I offered was not acceptable to the shopkeeper, so I pretended to leave, knowing he would call me back and quote a lower price.

As I expected, he called me back and lowered the price, although it was still much higher than what I was willing to pay. But as I was turning from the door to re-enter the shop, a picture frame caught my attention. Could it be? No, no it couldn't. I shook my head as if to clear my brain and my eyes. "And this frame, how much is it?" I asked.

The shopkeeper, interested in selling the brooch and the frame at the same time, said, "It is an excellent frame, sir—it is antique. If you will buy it, I'll give you a very good price. I assure you it is antique, at least one hundred years old. It is made of the wood of the olive tree. You cannot find another one similar to this, even if you search the whole bazaar…" He kept talking, determined to make a sale, but I don't remember what else he said because I was staring at the frame, mesmerized. Lacquered in black, it had gold-plated beads all around it. This was the same frame that hung in our living room for as long as my grandmother was alive. How could I be so positive? My grandfather's photograph was still in that frame.

That framed photograph was one of the three items that my grandmother had taken with her when she left Salonika after the Balkan War in 1913. She was the eldest daughter of a *petit bourgeois* family that had resided in that city for at least five generations. A widow with three children, she had been able to earn sufficient income as a dressmaker to provide for her family. After the Greek army occupied Salonika, she was afraid to remain and wanted to go to the Ottoman lands. When she left, she took the key to her house, her dead husband's framed photograph, and a portable sewing machine, the three most essential and prized items she possessed. Since she was going to return to Salonika—for it was inconceivable that the Empire would leave the pearl of the Aegean to the Greeks—she took the key to her house. After her husband died, she had kept his photograph, dusted it, cleaned it, and looked at it for hours. She could not leave it in an empty house that would become dusty in time. No matter where she and her children lived, she would continue to do what she knew best, dressmaking, so her sewing machine was absolutely necessary.

"How and when did you acquire this frame?" I asked the shopkeeper.

"Oh," he said, "I really don't know. About a year ago or so, I guess." He stopped for a moment and looked at the ceiling as if the ceiling was going to help him remember. "Yes," he continued, "about a year ago or so, someone brought this frame and an antique sewing machine. I sold it, a real antique it was, within a week. But I am stuck with this frame. Give me a good price and it is yours."

This picture and frame was the last legacy of my grandmother—the last legacy of my grandmother and her Salonika. It was always "beloved Salonika" for her; it could have been a blemished or spoiled city, perhaps even a poor, bankrupt one, but in her memory, distorted with time, it was beloved. Nostalgic remembrances do distort reality and can play the cruelest jokes on people who leave their native land by force, never to return. In time, fantasy overtakes the reality. Memories become gold-plated residues much closer to fantasy, and reality retreats.

For me, my grandmother's beloved Salonika was just a city in Greece, though in my boyhood I had heard so many descriptions and stories about it. I thought for what seemed to be a very long moment. Should I take the frame with me to America? But what for? For what purpose? I needed nothing more to remind me of my own beloved city. My house was full of Turkish carpets and decorated with the beautiful tiles for which the Ottomans were famous. My home was overflowing with books: books of poetry by Ottoman Turks with lace-like lines of Nedim, whose poems are closer to music than a string of rhymed words; the almost masochistic suffering of Fuzuli; the poems of Ruhi that ridicule the falsely pious, the despotic rulers, and the despised earthly goods; the best poems of republican Turks, like Ahmet Haşim, Nazım Hikmet, and Orhan Veli. The pitcher I used and the glasses from which I drank carried the sweet breezes of Istanbul. I listened to the best Ottoman music on my record player and talked to my wife in the language I loved the most.

I paid the price and bought the frame. Looking at the shopkeeper I said, "Now, break it."

He must have thought I was crazy. "Sir, you paid so much…"

I cut him short. "Break it," I said, "break it right now, here, in front of me." He looked at my face and was stupefied for a moment, but looking into my eyes and perhaps thinking that he saw a madman, he obliged.

Maybe it was a moment of madness, a moment of irrationality—but it was a moment I do not regret. Only afterward did I comprehend the rationality of my irrationality. For the truth was, I did not want the frame; I did not want the legacy of my grandmother; I did not want the inheritance of my aunt; I did not want the past. Yet I could not bring myself to leave the frame there to be bought by some *nouveau riche* just to adorn the wall of his house. The frame belonged to the past. Maybe I killed my grandmother finally for the third time. Maybe I was mad for a moment. Then and there, I confronted something that for years I had refused to acknowledge and accept. I was just a visitor in Turkey and I was bound to remain so until my dying day.

The next day I left Istanbul, the city to which I had said farewell so many times.

2
Roots

I

I know very little about my roots, much less about my forefathers beyond my grandparents. There are no photographs, no documents, and no family tree that traces the previous four or five generations. Traditionally in Muslim families, the only document, so to speak, is the last page of the family Koran where births and deaths are noted. This holy book was left behind, as everything else was, when my father's family escaped from Monastir and my mother's family had to depart from Salonika. To be uprooted was a personal tragedy for both families, a trauma that subsided in time, I imagine, but never totally disappeared.

Two families in two Balkan cities were totally uprooted as a result of a bloody war. Both were mere drops in the swelling stream of refugees, and the point of confluence for both was Istanbul, where my father would meet my mother, where they would marry, and where I would be born. I will pick up my parents' marriage and my life in Istanbul in due course. Let me get back to my roots.

From my father's side I am from Monastir, and from my mother's side I am from Salonika. I never knew my grandfathers since they had passed away long before I was born. My grandmothers have repeatedly told me that these two cities are my roots. Yet I do not belong to either of these cities. Save for a couple of pictures in travel books, I have never seen them. My roots do not go beyond myself, beyond Istanbul, my beloved city.

My grandmothers' tales, which I heard as a child even before entering primary school, were, for me, just some stories of their beloved cities. Because of my respect for my elders—a code of conduct drilled into every Turkish child—I listened to them time and again without interrupting and without expressing the boredom I felt from constantly hearing their endless laments of what was lost, their suffering caused by being evicted from their homelands. I was much too young to feel and understand their torment. Had I been older, I could have understood and appreciated much more. I could have asked all sorts of questions to discover their past, to comprehend how drastic was the move from a comfortable life to adopting a new life in a new country. Now, looking back many years later, I can only put together, with rudimentary bits and pieces buried in my memory, how bitter and unhappy they must have been. Yet they tried to make the most of what the new circumstances offered.

When I was in the fifth grade of the primary school, one subject I had to study was the history of the Ottoman Empire. I loved it. The glorious years of conquest, the Janissaries camping at the outskirts of Vienna were as much entertainment for me as the movies I used to see. Captain Blood or the Three Musketeers were like glorious Ottoman soldiers conquering the world. But as our curriculum covered decades and centuries of events, history became gloomier and gloomier. Wars and defeats were followed by more wars and more defeats.

At the beginning of the twentieth century, the glorious empire lay on its deathbed. Then the Balkan War began and ended, and the Ottoman lands in the Balkans were lost to the Greeks, Serbs, and Bulgarians. Cities such as Salonika, Monastir, and Skopje were lost forever. The Errol Flynns and Douglas Fairbanks Jr. disappeared and were replaced by my grandfathers and my grandmothers.

Salonika and Monastir. Only gradually have those names become real cities for me. Looking back, I realize that I became conscious of the fact that I was the descendant of two families weeded out from their land, from their houses, and forced to become poor and destitute refugees in a new city, the name of which they had heard but did not know. Now they are no longer stories told in my preschool years to keep me from doing any mischief. Reflecting, I understand only now their pain and sorrow, their yearnings for their native lands they were destined never to see. When I was in fifth grade, how could I possibly relate to what they were feeling?

How could I think or dream that I, too, was to someday become an immigrant, if not a refugee? But their stories must have remained in a corner of my memory just gathering dust.

Now, so many years later, I would like to take them out of their dusty corner and repeat them to myself in black and white. I cannot repeat the events contained in the stories told when I was a child word by word and chronologically. Nor can I do justice to the laments and sighs of the two old ladies who loved me, who nursed me, and who also hoped the best of all futures for me. At the end of their sad stories, both used to say: "The world forgot us. Our government forgot us. But you won't, will you?" Both looked forward to the day when I would join the army, recapture their native cities, and vindicate them. I can only do so with the lines I write.

I have no photographs of my paternal grandparents. My grandfather died long before I was born and I doubt very much if my paternal grandmother was ever photographed. The only picture of her is in my memory, as I see her round face and her spotlessly clean, white headscarf as she told me her story. She died when I was ten or eleven years old, three years after the death of my father. Despite my innocent young age, her sad face remains with me forever. I suspect she was never able to overcome her losses, including the death of her youngest son, my father, at the age of thirty-four.

I lived with my maternal grandmother until her death. Only one single photograph remains of my maternal grandparents. It is a photograph in which my grandmother looks sadly at a photograph of her husband, buried in Salonika before the family left the city. It also is the only photograph of my grandmother.

I may not remember everything, but I will try to narrate all that I remember.

II

My father was born in Monastir and given the name Sedat, meaning righteous, by my grandfather, Ali Rıza. My father remembered very little about the city where he was born; even if he had, he didn't have enough time to tell me, for he died when I was barely six years old. And I rarely saw him because my parents divorced when I was even younger.

From my grandmother's description, my grandfather must have been a very handsome man. "He was just like your father," she used to say. "Same handsome face, same dark blue eyes, except that he was taller and stockier."

I saw my grandmother very seldom; my father took me to her house only on religious holidays. My mother never accompanied us, for there was not much love lost between the two. My grandmother lived with my aunt, which was quite a distance from us. It took two streetcar trips and a boat trip, a journey of a good two hours, to get to her house. There, during these visits, I listened to her stories about her beloved city, Monastir, and their escape. When I first knew my grandmother, she had been physically living in Istanbul for very many years, but her mind was always in Monastir. She told me about Monastir time and time again. It was her beloved city. What follows is her story.

For my grandmother, Monastir—today known as Bitola—was a Turkish city from time immemorial. Of course, I never corrected her; actually, it had become an Ottoman city in the fifteenth century. "It is a biiiiig city," she used to say, emphasizing and stretching the word as much as she could. Indeed it was, with more than half a million inhabitants, mostly Turkish but with a large minority of Greeks, Bulgarians, Albanians, and Serbs, who lived together harmoniously and peacefully. "Like many rose buds of different colors on the same bush" was her favorite expression. A river ran through the city that hustled and bustled, for it was the seat of the provincial government, a military academy, and an army corps. It was full of mosques, churches, schools, and shops. It was a rich city, agriculturally as well as commercially; in the wide valley where it was situated they grew wheat, barley, and oats.

"They were taller than men when their spikes turned golden yellow under the hot August sun," my grandmother used to say, her sorrowful eyes wandering around the poorly furnished room. "Don't look at us now, we were rich then." How rich, I do not know, but certainly she had lived a life much richer and much more comfortable than the one she had in Istanbul, the city of her last stop.

And then, in 1912, came the First Balkan War, engulfing the Ottoman Balkans in fire and blood. Tragic news reached Monastir from the towns and villages occupied by the Serbian forces much faster than the Serbs themselves, although they, too, were rapidly advancing. Serbian soldiers, as well as armed irregulars, were killing local soldiers and citizens alike, burning crops and raping young girls and boys. Ethnic cleansing was in full swing. The Greeks and the Serbs, who had lived peacefully and amicably as good neighbors, suddenly turned against the Muslim Turks. Stories of calamities mixed with truth and exaggerations circulated in Monastir, sowing seeds of fear and desperation into the hearts of its population. Fearful for the safety of his family, my grandfather, Ali Rıza, left Monastir in a hurry. That was the beginning of my grandmother's story, which I listened to so many times that I can relate it today as if I had lived it personally.

"Our army did not defend us and retreated in a hurry," she would continue. "We were left defenseless; we were betrayed. Your grandfather placed in a horse-drawn wagon a mattress and a few cushions for our comfort, for me, for your aunts, and for your father, and in a hurry we followed the retreating Ottoman soldiers."

Ali Rıza had been a prosperous farmer in Monastir. He owned a sizeable tract of land on which he had cultivated wheat. "You could not traverse from one end of our land to the other in one day," my grandmother used to say. "Our large house was right at the center of the city. Dozens of peasants worked on our land, sowing in the spring and harvesting at the end of the summer. Wheat used to earn us lots of money."

Winter came to Monastir shortly after the harvest months and stayed until early spring. "The long winter months were the most enjoyable time for us. My Ali Rıza"—she always referred to her husband as "my Ali Rıza"—"sat all day long in front of the fireplace, sipping his strong tea and smoking his long-stemmed pipe filled with golden Balkan tobacco." According to her, my grandfather loved to smoke. Every spring he separated a small patch of land to cultivate tobacco purely for his own consumption, a patch he worked with tender, loving care. He alone sowed it, watched it grow, harvested it, dried the leaves, and cut them in very tiny strips. No one was allowed to touch his tobacco.

After the long and arduous months of spring and summer, winter was for pleasure only. My father and my aunts ran up and down the stairs and chased each other in the corridors, the wooden floors squeaking under their feet. My grandmother, who was of Albanian stock, sang beautiful Albanian folk songs with a wonderful soprano voice while preparing her husband's favorite dishes in the kitchen. The entire family gathered in the living room during the long nights, children played, Ali Rıza smoked his pipe, and his wife continually refreshed his cup with black tea. Life was wonderful in Monastir.

When there was no more snow on the ground, it was once again time to till the soil. Ali Rıza worked on his land with dozens of workers, supervised their work, and watched his wheat grow inch by inch, its color turning from pale green to emerald and then to golden yellow. Soon it would be harvest time. Razor sharp scythes and sickles, hand tools, were used to cut the crop. Ali Rıza took his harvest to the market and returned home, his pockets bulging with gold coins. Then it was time once again to get ready for winter. His wife made butter from the milk of their cows, while Ali Rıza stocked the pantry with rice, beans, olive oil, pastrami, pickles, and a variety of dried fruits and nuts. He also made sure that there was enough firewood to last the entire winter and waited impatiently for the fall of the first snow.

All those days were now behind him. Nothing tangible was left, except his family and a horse-drawn wagon. He left behind his un-harvested wheat, his tobacco patch, his large and comfortable house, and his land. It is an old Turkish proverb that says that a farmer who leaves his land also leaves behind his soul. The land was not worth having if the price was to live under Serbian occupation. The road would to take him to Salonika.

"I will stop there," he said to himself. "Our sultan would never leave Salonika to the Infidels." He decided that, after a brief pause in that city, he would reload his wagon and restart his journey toward Istanbul. Salonika's days would be numbered, too. Soon after the fall of Monastir to the Serbs, Salonika fell to the Greeks.

At first, he followed the retreating army on the road to Salonika. But soon the road became crowded with hundreds of refugees and he began to lag behind. It rained incessantly, and the road quickly turned to mud—a cold, viscous trap. His wagon got stuck in the thick mire many a time. His poor horse, nose covered with white foam, tried to pull the wagon. When the horse couldn't move, Ali

Rıza pulled and freed the wagon with superhuman effort. They had to reach Salonika before the Serbian army caught up with them. The tide of an ever-growing human flood swelled on the road with them. There were peasants with their two-wheeled carts loaded with people, chairs, pots and pans, sometimes even a goat or two. Peasants carried their babies in their arms, or their grandparents on their backs, escaping from the enemy, in knee-high mud, walking toward Salonika, a city they had heard about but had never seen. The sorrow of being uprooted from their land and the fear of the unknown were two inerasable seals stamped on their faces.

Not only Ali Rıza, but everybody on the road showed superhuman efforts. The wounded soldiers of a defeated, demoralized army, with blood-stained bandages, using their rifles as sticks, tried to catch up with their comrades, begging the passing wagons and carts for a lift. Ali Rıza closed his eyes and shut his ears. There was no room on a one-horse-drawn wagon. He had to take his family to safety. Helplessness brought tears to his eyes, mixing with the rain as they ran down his cheeks.

The last bastion of the empire in the Balkans, Salonika, fell to the Greeks only a few months after Ali Rıza and his family arrived. Blue and white flags were everywhere. Ali Rıza took his family, his wagon, and his horse and once again took to the road, this time toward Istanbul. His hopes had been dashed. The sultan had left the pearl of the Aegean to the enemy.

For Ali Rıza, Istanbul was a strange place, stranger than Salonika. Having spent most of the money he had taken with him in Salonika, he was completely drained by the time he arrived in Istanbul. He sold his gold watch and chain, and with the proceeds managed to rent two rooms in a poor district of Istanbul. He had no money, no home of his own, and no fireplace, which he sorely missed. His prospects of earning money were dim, for the city was full of other Balkan refugees just like him, wearing their baggy trousers and red fezzes on which green muslin was wrapped. They were all looking for jobs and were willing to do anything for a pittance. They all looked alike, with their sullen faces and yellowish complexions that shouted hunger to every passer-by.

Ali Rıza was just one among thousands. His only thought was to earn some money for their daily bread. He tried not to think about his oldest daughter, who had a personal maid when growing up as a fragile girl in Monastir, as she began working as a maid in the home of a rich family. He tried not to think of Monastir at all, not of his land or of his house. A refugee must leave everything behind, even memories he tries to forget, since to think of them is so painful.

He left his home early every morning to hunt for a job. His desperate struggle for a loaf of bread was more of a failure than a success. The prosperous farmer of Monastir was reduced to accepting any job—cleaning latrines, washing windows, digging ditches. He tried everything short of begging. Even when he did not find any job, he waited until the evening to return home so that there would be one less mouth to feed at lunch. He was so confused, so grief-stricken, that sometimes he lost his way back home. He wandered with unending anxiety, lost in the unfamiliar streets for hours until he finally found the right street. The rain poured, the wind howled.

One rainy evening, Ali Rıza returned home soaking wet and empty-handed, not even a loaf of bread under his arm. He barely managed to walk upstairs. As he opened the door to his bedroom, he pressed his hand on his heart and collapsed. As soon as he examined him, the doctor said "cardiac arrest." My grandmother often said: "My Ali Rıza died of a broken heart."

One month after the death of Ali Rıza, the Ottoman government threw the country into the fires of the First World War. The day general mobilization was declared, Sedat—my father—had turned sixteen, two years short of the age of compulsory conscription.

III

The city of Salonika was the "Pearl of the Aegean" in Ottoman times. A Byzantine city until it was captured by the Ottoman Turks in 1430; it had remained a minor port, somewhat larger than a fishing village, until Isabel and Ferdinand expelled all the Jews from the Iberian Peninsula. Apparently a wise Ottoman sultan had once said, "Spain's loss is our gain; let us bring all the Jews to the Ottoman land." He sent a flotilla to bring all those who accepted his invitation and gave them refuge, primarily in three Ottoman cities: Istanbul, Izmir, and Salonika. With them they brought their advanced knowledge, their financial wizardry, and their printing technology. Most of the Spanish Jews settled in Salonika, some in nearby towns. They were to transform Salonika into a commercial hub and a cultural center in less than a century.

Salonika reached its zenith in the nineteenth century with a mixture of European and Eastern life and culture. It was a metropolis second only to Istanbul. Wide avenues; a modern port; running water in the houses; streetcars crisscrossing the city; theaters; schools and higher learning institutions; military academies; numerous factories; and rich and varied cultures of Turks, Albanians, Greeks, Bulgarians, and Sephardic Jews speaking a curious mixture of Turkish and medieval Spanish—all these things gave the city, with its mosques, synagogues, and churches, the look of a harmonious Tower of Babel. It was a city of gardens, white-washed walls, green shutters, and red-tiled roofs. My maternal grandmother, Aisha, always called it "my beloved city."

She was born in Salonika, as were her mother, father, and perhaps her ancestors going back three hundred years. Grandmother Aisha was born in the second half of the nineteenth century. She never knew her exact birth date. She used to say "I was a little girl when the kidnapping of the Christian girl caused quite a scare." One Christian girl had fallen in love with a Muslim youth, converted to Islam, and had taken refuge in a house. Her co-religionists had forced her out of the house, and a melée ensued with the Turks. Trying to stop the escalating brawl, the French and German consuls intervened; both were killed.

For the European powers, this was a legitimate excuse to meddle in the internal affairs of the "sick man of Europe," as they called the Ottoman Empire. They sent warships to the harbor of Salonika that trained their cannons upon the city. Aisha often said, "With my father, I watched the warships from the balcony of our house. I was a little girl." Since this incident took place in 1876 and my grandmother was a little girl at the time, she must have been born in the early 1870s.

Aisha's father was a well-to-do businessman. She never went to school, never learned to read and write. For a girl in a rather conservative household, those things were not necessary. She learned, and learned well, to cook, to sew, and to raise children. Being the eldest child in the family, she was the helping hand of her mother, tending to her younger brothers and sisters.

She married, according to the customs, by arrangement among families. She fell in love with her husband when she saw him for the first time on their nuptial night. She felt she was the happiest of all the girls she knew. She gave birth to one boy and three girls. The next to the last daughter, Atiye, was destined to be my mother.

Aisha's happiness did not last long. Her husband succumbed to lung cancer in the seventh year of their marriage. That was the first tragedy in her life. The second, the Balkan War of 1912-1913, was not far away. Because the Ottoman army was expected to counterattack and retake the city, she and her family did not leave right away. Of course, the army failed. One incident forced Aisha and her children to flee the city.

I listened to her story maybe a hundred times or more. She used to say, "It was Atiye's fault. It was because of her that we fled." I remember all the minute details of my mother's so-called fault.

One afternoon, after returning from school, Atiye kept pestering her mother to take her to the market to buy a new notebook. Her mother reminded her that it was late in the afternoon and by the time they went down to the center of the city and returned it would be too late and too dark. They could not dare to return home after dark, for the city was under Greek occupation; it was dangerous to be out at night, and only God knew what would happen with soldiers roaming in the streets. Atiye began to cry; the only remedy children know to soften the hearts of their mothers. Her mother did not give in. The answer was No!

Atiye insisted. "But our teacher said that we had to come tomorrow with a new notebook. Please, Mom."

Her mother retorted, "Look, tell your teacher that your mother was sick and could not go to the market. Tomorrow I'll go early in the morning and I'll buy what you want, all right?"

That was no consolation for Atiye. With her teenage logic she counterattacked. "But Mom, you always tell us not to lie. How am I going to tell my teacher that you were sick when you are not sick? I do not want to tell a lie."

As the crying got louder, Aisha, out of desperation and frustration, lifted her hand to slap Atiye's face, but stopped. She was the one who had always told her children not to lie under any circumstance, and now she was encouraging a lie.

"Oh, shush," she said, "let's go. Leave your youngest sister with the neighbor and tell your elder sister to get ready. Let's go quickly and don't forget to tell your sister to put her veil on."

Three women, two veiled and one unveiled, left the house, turned the corner, and went toward the market with quick steps.

Aisha had good reason to be apprehensive about going to the market. The Greek army had occupied Salonika only a few months earlier and, as is usual with all occupying forces, their behavior was antagonistic toward those who were occupied. There were rumors of rape, summary arrests, and executions. The Muslim population of Salonika lived in fear.

With her young husband dead, Aisha was alone in her home with three daughters and a teenage son. She was trying to survive by sewing dresses for the neighbors; these modest earnings supplemented what her brother gave her from the family business.

She belonged to an old petit bourgeois family of Salonika that had lived there for many generations. Aisha's great-grandfather had started a family business. After the death of her father, her younger brother had taken over the business. He helped Aisha financially and she respected him in every way. Now, during the Greek occupation, the business was not doing very well; still, he was optimistic that the Ottoman army would liberate Salonika and the bad times would be over soon. But months had passed and when the peace treaty was signed, Salonika was left to the Greeks, permanently. The occupying forces began to behave like conquerors.

The three women entered the first shop they saw and purchased the notebook that Atiye wanted. Dusk had set in and hardly anybody was on the street. Walking toward home through dimly lit streets, they heard footsteps quickly approaching. Soon two young Greek soldiers caught up with them and began to walk next to Aisha. She was terrified, yet she did not change the pace of her walking; she simply muttered to her daughters, "Don't say a word."

A few minutes passed before one of the soldiers spoke; those few minutes felt like hours. In broken Turkish, one soldier turned to Aisha. "Madam, we come to you tonight, but kurichi. Yes?"

Aisha knew a few words of Greek to understand that those two soldiers were after the girls. For the rest of her life, she hated to remember what she felt at that moment. Almost in a daze, and with the instinct of a lioness defending her cubs, she turned to one of them and shouted, "You come to me. But for my kurichi, for my girls, you just go to hell, you sons of bitches."

She took a step back and with lightning speed kicked one of the soldier's balls with all her might. Lo and behold, the soldiers, instead of becoming aggressive and belligerent, opted to turn the first corner and disappear. Aisha was trembling with anger and fear. The three women knocked on the door of the first house they saw. No sooner had they entered the neighbor's house than Aisha fainted.

Early the next morning, Aisha went to see her brother and told him exactly what had happened the evening before. He looked worried. He was indeed at an impasse to find a way to protect his sister. As was his habit, he first lit a cigarette and began to talk with measured words.

"I understand, my dear, I understand your fear and concern. The situation is far from being an accident. We do not know whether those soldiers really ran away or will case the neighborhood until they identify your house. If they do, may God protect us. You are alone in your house. You have no husband to protect you, and your son is still a teenager. That is not much of a comfort. I am here for you always, but I am not always with you."

He stopped for a while. Aisha did not know what to say. She had always abided by the decisions of her brother, especially after the death of her husband. She sat there silently, watching him, waiting for him to continue. She did not have to wait long.

"You know, now that the peace treaty has been signed, Salonika is a Greek city and there is no hope that our army will return."

He had a sad expression on his face. Aisha looked at him lovingly. "What are we going to do?" She had no idea what could be done.

"We have to leave. That can be done, and that is what we will do."

Aisha could not believe her ears. To leave Salonika where her family had lived for hundreds of years? Her whole world was Salonika. Where would they go? She was stupefied.

Her brother saw the bewilderment in his sister's eyes. "I have been thinking about it for some time. The only place where we can go is Istanbul."

Step by step, he explained his plan to his sister. First Aisha and her four children would leave for Izmir; Aisha's four sisters would follow later on. He would stay behind in Salonika to liquidate whatever remained of the family business, and then join them with his family and start all over again. He would buy tickets for Aisha and the children and give her money to tide her over in Izmir until he arrived. He would also give her letters addressed to his business associates in Izmir to ensure that they looked after her and her children.

Aisha left her brother's house and returned home, confused and very unhappy. Now she had to pack. But pack what? Her brother had said that she had to be ready at a moment's notice. She could not believe that she would never return to Salonika; she simply refused to believe that. She was convinced that sooner or later the Ottoman army would recapture the city. Salonika could not possibly be left to the Greeks. She packed a few basic necessities, took down the picture of her late husband from the wall, caressed it and packed it together with the other belongings. And yes, also her sewing machine, her Ottoman brand sewing machine that had served her faithfully. "All is left but the key to the house," she muttered. "When I leave I must not forget the key to the house."

Her brother came to see her off at the quay. The boat that was to take her and her children to Izmir was getting ready to sail. Farewell, Salonika, goodbye friends, goodbye memories, goodbye the grave of her husband.

A fog like white gauze descended upon the city as the boat left the harbor. She called her children to the deck.

"Look, children," she said, "this is our city and one day we shall return," insh'allah she murmured and dried her wet eyes.

They never returned. Neither Aisha nor the children saw Salonika, their beloved city, again.

IV

On the second morning after the boat's departure from Salonika, the sun shone brightly with not a single cloud in the sky. There was barely a breeze on the dark blue Aegean Sea, and Izmir was less than one day away. My grandmother, Aisha, awoke early on the upper deck; her children were still sleeping on makeshift beds, and nothing stirred on the deck. Quietly she walked around the sleeping Balkan refugees and entered the restroom.

As she was about to leave, her foot touched something that she thought was a belt. She bent down and picked it up. It was a very heavy money belt filled with gold coins. Bewildered, she was unsure what to do. Should she leave it there for the rightful owner to come and find it? Perhaps someone else would come and take it instead. With that thought she took the belt, tied it under her skirt, and returned to where her children were sleeping. Squatting down, she lowered her veil and began to carefully observe the people on deck.

It was early and most people were still sleeping, but then one by one the passengers, mostly Balkan peasants escaping from the Serbs, Greeks, and Bulgarians, began to wake up. Suddenly she noticed a middle-aged man, typically dressed like a peasant in a pair of baggy trousers called shalwar, a colorful shirt and a red fez on his head, running toward the restroom. He entered and quickly came out. He was not running anymore; he was wandering aimlessly on the deck, sobbing with tears running down his cheeks and repeatedly and almost imperceptibly murmuring, "I am dead, I am dead."

Aisha wondered: could he be the owner of the belt? She walked toward him, lifted her veil, smiled, and said, "Good morning, brother. Is something ailing you? Can I be of assistance?"

The man looked at her and told her his misfortune. He was from one of the villages near Salonika. He and his family were running away from the Greek army and going to Izmir. He had three teenage daughters. They had left behind their land and their house. He was a man of some means; he had money. He stood silent for a moment and then continued, "All my money was in my money belt. I went to the restroom for ablution before the Morning Prayer and I must have dropped the belt there. I went back to the restroom just now, but the belt was not there. How am I going to take care of my family? I wish I were dead."

His cry was now audible almost all over the entire deck. Aisha calmly said to the man, "Stop crying, brother. I found a money belt in the restroom. Tell me how much money you had in it. If your answer is correct, the belt is yours."

"Ninety-eight coins. Initially I had one hundred coins, but I spent one in Salonika and with the second I bought the boat tickets for me and my family."

He continued to sob non-stop, repeating, "I am dead."

Aisha undid the belt from under her skirt, emptied it, and counted the coins. There were ninety-eight as the man had said. "Here," she said, "take your belt, it is yours."

The man was dumbfounded. He stopped sobbing but did not know what to say. Aisha turned around and started to walk toward her sleeping children. The man ran after her.

"Stop, sister," he cried, "stop and accept these five gold pieces with my thanks."

The tears were still running down his cheeks but he was smiling. Aisha refused his offer. She had done what any honest person would have done. Honesty had no price for her. She squatted next to her children and murmured a religious maxim that was drilled into her since her early age, "God helps the righteous."

At that moment, a well-dressed man with gold-rimmed glasses, a gold chain hanging on his waistcoat, and a cane with an ivory grip in his hand appeared in front of her. She looked at him and wondered who he could be. Maybe a rich merchant. The man spoke before she could utter a word.

"Good morning, sister. Please forgive me, but I just saw what transpired between you and that man. I was impressed by your honesty. Who are you? Where are you coming from and where are you going? By the way, I am the governor of the Adana province."

And he gave his name.

Aisha told the governor her story. She belonged to a well-established trader family in Salonika. She had lost her husband some years back and now she and her children were escaping from the Greek occupation. They were heading to Izmir where her brother had business associates. Hopefully, with their help, she would be able to settle there, albeit temporarily.

The governor listened to her without interruption. Aisha's four children were all awake and standing behind her. She presented them to the governor. "This is my son, Ismail, and these are my three daughters, Celile, Atiye, Emine."

"Well, that is good," said the governor. "I wish the best for all of you, honest lady. I would like to invite you to my cabin for breakfast. Please accept my invitation, together with the children, of course."

The governor's cabin was large, quite luxurious, and a welcome change from the deck. As soon as they settled down, he rang the bell for the cabin boy and ordered tea, toast, butter, and jam. Aisha made sure that the children behaved properly. Following the custom, they did not speak during breakfast, which they ate hungrily and quickly. Aisha did not speak either, for the man was a governor, obviously a very important person judging from his outfit and his cabin.

The silence continued until the breakfast was over. The governor appeared to be in a pensive mood. He spoke first. "Dear sister, you are planning to go to Izmir, a city where you know nobody. I understand that your brother has business associates there. All the same, they are strangers to you and you are a stranger to them. I would like to make an offer to you. Why don't you come with me to Adana?"

Aisha was taken aback. She had never heard of a city called Adana. The governor looked very honorable, but what could he have in mind and what could she do in Adana? She looked inquisitively into his eyes.

It was not difficult for the governor to guess what was crossing Aisha's mind. "Don't worry," he said. "I suggest the following. I need grade school teachers in Adana and I have great difficulty finding them. As you know, times are not good at all. There is a talk of war in Europe, and our government has declared partial mobilization. You would be much better off if you were in the heart of Anatolia instead of Izmir. This is what I propose. I can provide teaching jobs for your two daughters. The third one is much too young. You, dear sister, you can teach sewing to the fourth and fifth graders; your daughters, Celile and Atiye, can teach reading and writing. I have a modern grade school for girls right in the center of the city and I have no teachers. What do you say, sister?"

Aisha was confused. "I don't know," she said. "I don't know."

"I understand," said the governor, "you may think that my offer is tactless perhaps, but believe me it is honest, as honest, sister, as your honesty a little while ago. Let me leave you by yourselves for a little while. Talk it over. If you decide to accept my offer, I will see to it that your tickets are extended until Adana at no cost to you. And believe me, you will be much better off in Adana than in Izmir."

He took his walking stick, walked out, and left Aisha and her children in the cabin. The heavy air was almost visible in the cabin. Aisha was at a loss; never before in her life had she made a decision by herself. Her husband had made all the necessary decisions, and, after his death, she had relied on her brother whenever the necessity arose. In fact, it was her brother who had insisted that they leave Salonika. Now, all alone, she had to make a decision for herself and for her children. A few minutes of silence felt like hours. Finally, she gathered her courage.

"Children, what do you think?"

Ismail, her son, at whom she looked when posing this question, answered, "We must go to Izmir. Didn't our uncle say so? We do not know who this man is. He says he is the governor, but who knows? Right?"

Her younger daughter, Atiye, did not share her brother's opinion. Attracted by the idea of being a teacher, she argued vehemently. "Why should we go to Izmir? We do not know a soul there. Why should we beg for help from people we do not know? We can earn our own bread with our own sweat."

Her older sister Celile echoed Atiye's words. The die was cast. As they were leaving the cabin Aisha repeated to herself silently, "God helps the righteous."

The boat stopped one whole day at Izmir to load and unload. The next day, it anchored in the bay of Mersin, a small coastal town on the eastern Mediterranean that served as port for the province of Adana. Since there was no wharf, it remained anchored in the bay and passengers were ferried to the shore in rowboats. Aisha and her children were among the first passengers to set foot on the land of Anatolia.

The governor had already disembarked and gave orders to his staff that had come to assist him. "Get me a two-horse coach for the teachers and send messengers galloping to Adana that the vice governor should find a good furnished house for them."

He also gave orders for the purchase of food and water, and two armed policemen to guard the teachers' coach. Soon, three coaches, one carrying the governor, another his staff, and the third Aisha and her children, were on their way to Adana.

Adana was a small agricultural town south of the Taurus Mountains, about one-third the size of Salonika. It was an old, sleepy city—most houses were no higher than one story and built of adobe. Except for the major streets, the roads were unpaved, dusty in the summer, muddy in the winter. Its population was mostly Turks, with some Kurds, Circassians, Arabs, Armenians, and Greeks. Aisha was disappointed with the looks of her new city, for it was nothing like her beautiful Salonika.

Aisha and her children settled in a completely furnished and well-prepared house that used to belong to an Armenian businessman who had taken refuge in another region of Anatolia. Skirmishes had flared up against the Armenians after an Armenian terrorist organization had thrown a bomb into the sultan's carriage in Istanbul in 1905. The sultan had escaped unscathed, but several members of his entourage were killed. There arose such an uncontrollable fury against the Armenians all over the empire that in Adana, where a relatively large Armenian minority lived, bloody clashes with Turkish gangs forced them to flee and find refuge elsewhere. Therefore, several uninhabited houses were available, and the vice governor had selected the best fully furnished one for the new teachers.

Aisha and her two daughters began their duties at once in the modern primary girls' school. Their life took a pleasant turn; they led a comfortable life for three years. Unfortunately, their comfort did not last long. The assassination of the Crown Prince of Austria sparked the First World War, whereupon Enver Pasha, the Minister of War and virtual dictator of the Ottoman Empire, signed a secret pact with Germany. Soon the country was plunged into fire and blood. Little did he know that by signing the pact with Germany, he was signing the death warrant of a nearly five-hundred-year-old empire.

With the declaration of full mobilization, Aisha's son, Ismail, was ordered to report to the induction center in Adana. He was barely seventeen and Aisha was afraid that the war was going to take him away. She was having nightmares, dreaming that either he returned maimed from the war or that she received a letter announcing his death.

Once again, the governor came to Aisha's help. He hired her son as a policeman. The police force was exempt from military duty, thus Ismail was spared. The war, however, brought difficulties galore. First, prices skyrocketed. Then came the shortage of foodstuff. Life in that small Anatolian city was no longer pleasant and tranquil. The news from the fronts was gloomy. Although the army had gloriously defended the Dardanelles, disaster reigned in the eastern and southern fronts. The battle with the Russians in the East was lost and the Turkish army that had crossed into Palestine and the Sinai Peninsula in order to recapture Egypt retreated. Ottoman cities like Jerusalem, Baghdad, and Damascus fell into the hands of the British army. Adana was on the brink of a panic.

On one of these particularly nerve-wracking days, the governor came to visit Aisha. His jovial manner had disappeared; in fact, he looked very gloomy. He was being transferred to the Bursa province at the northwest corner of Anatolia and was ordered to assume his duties there within a month.

"I think," he said, "it would be better if you were to move to Bursa as well. There I can reinstate you and your daughters as teachers and your son as a policeman. I do not know what will happen in Adana. The English army is moving north from Damascus and Adana might fall into the hands of the English, God forbid. The newly appointed governor does not know you and may not protect you at all. Of course, the decision is yours."

Once again, Aisha and her children were forced to move. They packed whatever they could. Once more, Aisha took her husband's framed picture, the sewing machine that helped her in the sewing classes in the school and provided additional income, and the key to her house in Salonika, to which she constantly hoped she would return one day. Once again, the family became refugees, this time in Bursa.

Bursa, the first capital of the Ottoman Empire, was a welcome change. It was situated at the foot of Mount Olympus, in a valley that was green as far as the eye could see, full of trees, historical buildings, mosques, libraries, and mausoleums. While the climate of Adana had been oppressive with winters of unending rains and scalding hot summers, Bursa was pleasant, with cool winters and warm sunshine during the summer. Aisha and her children settled into a nice house, her daughters began to teach in a girls' school, and her son was once again a policeman.

The war ended with disastrous results for the empire. Those who were responsible for the defeat took refuge in other countries, and those who collaborated with the previous dictatorial regime were suspected of misdeeds. The governor of Bursa was summarily dismissed. One early morning he came to visit Aisha. He was not the same confident man Aisha had met on the boat. He was sulking, his face was almost white, and his body stooped.

"It is all politics," he said. "The new government dismissed all the governors of the previous regime, and some have even been arrested. It is well known that I was a protégé of Enver Pasha. My future is bleak. It is also well known that in Bursa, you and your children have been under my protection."

Aisha was disturbed. With a trembling voice she asked, "What shall we do?"

"Leave Bursa, leave as soon as possible. Go to Istanbul. In that big city, no one will know who you are. Never tell anyone you knew me. Go as soon as you can."

He bid farewell to Aisha and murmured, "May God help you."

The suitcases were packed once again. As she did in all their previous moves, Aisha took her husband's picture, her sewing machine, and the key to her house in Salonika. After a short boat trip, they were in Istanbul, a city where they knew absolutely no one. It was their third place of refuge in four years, and it would be the last. They settled in a two-story house in the coastal district of Üsküdar. From a second floor window, one could see the port of Istanbul where the allied fleet of Britain, France, and Greece had anchored with the intention of occupying the city after the armistice was signed.

The Greek warship Averof had anchored closest to the shore of Üsküdar. Aisha would not set foot on the second floor. She could not bring herself to see the Greek flag hoisted at the aft of the ship. In 1923, after the nationalist army under the command of Mustafa Kemal Atatürk had freed the country from the occupation, and after the allied navy left Istanbul, Aisha looked at the Bosporus for the first time and nostalgically thought of the sea in her beautiful Salonika. Tears ran down her cheeks.

Neither my grandmother nor her children would be itinerant anymore. They all lived in Üsküdar until their dying days without ever returning to Salonika. Just before her death, my grandmother grabbed my hand and told me her last wish. She wanted to be buried with the key to her house that she had left behind in Salonika. I dutifully complied with her wish.

3
Born in Istanbul

I

After three years of blood and fire, the nationalist army succeeded in defeating the Greek and Allied forces that had occupied half of Turkey, still the Ottoman Empire then. Subsequently, the sultanate and caliphate were abolished, the republic was declared, and reforms followed one another with the intention of freeing the country from all the vestiges of the old regime. The civil law was modeled upon the Swiss code, polygamy was outlawed, state and religion was completely separated, and secularism was declared. Another fundamental reform in the making was the change of the alphabet from the Arabic-based script to the Latin-based one.

In one of the early years of the republic, a young grade school teacher—Atiye, my mother—sat on the window side of the ferry crossing the Bosporus. She was returning from an interview at the Office of the Directorate of Public Education, where she had been told that she was chosen as one of the principal persons to lead the new alphabet campaign in her neighborhood. She was to attend a week-long crash course and thereafter teach the new alphabet not only to her students, but in the evening, when she was to hold courses for anyone in her neighborhood who was willing to learn it. These courses were to last one whole month.

She felt immensely honored and excited by this new task, which gave her a great deal of responsibility, yet at the same time, she was a bit anxious at this undertaking. To be one of the soldiers in the campaign of modernization, to contribute, albeit modestly, to Atatürk's endeavors, was a great honor indeed. But the responsibility of teaching the new alphabet to her students in a couple of weeks during the day and to the young and the old during the night could be an insurmountable task. Since she knew some French that she had learned in her school in Salonika, learning the new alphabet was a cinch for her, but for the others in the neighborhood?

She was so full of joy and apprehension that she could not read the newspaper she bought at the ferry boat station. She looked at the words and sentences, but she was having difficulty understanding what she thought she was reading. Her mind was elsewhere. The memories of the past and the unknown future were intertwined in her head. Escaping from Salonika and the Balkan War with her widowed mother, brother, and sisters; moving from one city to another in Anatolia; her mother's superhuman efforts to provide a livelihood for her children by sewing dresses with her rickety old sewing machine; the disastrous First World War; beginning her teaching career when she was only fifteen due to the shortage of manpower during the war; the final move to Istanbul; studying day and night for the qualifying examination to become a bonafide school teacher; her appointment to a grade school in Üsküdar; her new task to teach the Latin-based Turkish alphabet; the reaction of those who were to attend the evening courses; her desire to succeed in her new task—all of those thoughts whirled in front of her eyes like a macabre dance.

She glanced at the headlines of the paper: the new alphabet would be introduced in the coming academic year. She folded the paper and fixed her eyes on the white-crested blue waves, totally oblivious to her surroundings. She was completely unaware that two rather conservatively clad middle-aged ladies were looking at her intensely. The older of the two turned her head to her companion.

"Do you notice the young lady who is sitting in front of us?"

"Yes, you mean the one with the grey two-piece suit who is reading the paper, right?"

"Right, I have noticed her, too. She is not very beautiful, but she looks nice and charming. What have you in mind?"

"Same thing as you—she would be a perfect bride for our brother, Sedat. I wonder whether she is married."

"No way to know, she is wearing gloves."

Their whispered conversation continued throughout the fifteen-minute ferry ride. As they left the ferry, they decided to follow the young lady in the grey two-piece suit to find out where she lived. They had agreed there and then that she might be a good match for their brother, who was divorced after a short and unhappy marriage.

Fairly early on a Friday morning, still a day off in Turkey (which changed to Sunday a few years later), the two ladies from the ferry rang the doorbell where Atiye lived. It was a hot and humid August day. Atiye opened the door and found two ladies smiling at her rather timidly. The older one spoke first.

"Sorry to disturb you, my girl, we are tired and very thirsty. Could you give us a glass of water?"

An innocent request indeed! The custom of the land, a centuries-old tradition based on Muslim religion, dictates that one cannot deny water to anyone.

"Of course," answered Atiye, "please come in and rest a while."

The two ladies eagerly accepted the invitation. When Atiye went to the kitchen to fetch the water one of the ladies said to the other, "Did you notice, sister? She has no ring on her finger."

They both smiled. Atiye returned to the living room with two glasses of water and two cups of coffee, a common courtesy in a Turkish household.

While they were having coffee, the two ladies engaged Atiye in a seemingly innocent conversation. How old was she? What did she do? Where was she from? They seemed to be pleased with the answers they received, especially when Atiye said that she and her family were from Salonika. The older one seemed especially pleased.

"Aah," she said, "from the Balkans. Really? We also are from there, from Monastir. What a lovely city that was! The Balkan War made us refugees in Istanbul."

Indeed, they spoke with an unmistakable Balkan accent. They moved their heads from left to right as they spoke, rounding the "o"s into "u"s and ending their sentences with a sing song.

After a few minutes of silence the older one asked, "My beautiful girl, is your father at home?"

It was then Atiye knew why they had come. It was definitely not for a glass of water.

"My father passed away in Salonika before we left. Let me see whether my mother is up."

She left the room to wake her up. As she went up the stairs she saw her mother coming down.

"Mother," she said, "there are two ladies in the living room. They came with the pretext that they were thirsty, but their intention must be different. You go and talk to them. I am not marrying anyone this way." As a young progressive Turkish girl, Atiye was rebelling against the old custom of marriage through go-betweens.

"Kismet," said the mother.

Well, my mother married my father a few months later, and I was born just about two years thereafter on one of those bitter cold winter days of Istanbul in the middle of December, at five-thirty in the morning. For two days, the doctors were not sure whether I was going to survive. I did. And the third day my father registered me. My birth certificate reads as follows: Name: Fuat Metin: Father's name: Ali Sedat. Mother's name: Hatice Atiye. Country of birth: Turkey. City of birth: Istanbul. District: Üsküdar.

II

I have a faint memory of my father. I do not know when my mother and my father were married, nor do I know when they were divorced. My mother never spoke of him, never said any word either in favor of him or against him. She never told me, even in my adult years, the reason for their divorce. Whatever the reason was, she took it with her to her grave.

My grandmother did not speak favorably of him. For her, he was a no-good man. But I never knew why she had reached that conclusion. Nevertheless, my father visited me every other week. He always brought a box of chocolate. He was never allowed to take me out for walks, to go to the seaside, or to the fair grounds. It was only twice a year, on the occasion of religious feasts, that he and I went out alone to visit his mother, my grandmother. The best memory I have of him is the arrangement of my circumcision. As a proud father, he took me, with my mother, to his tailor, ordered a dark blue suit that I was supposed to wear prior to the circumcision, and stayed at my bedside all night long after the operation was performed. That was the last I saw him. About a month later, I was told that he had died.

Despite the fact that I grew up without a father, I did not have an unhappy childhood. I attended the grade school in our neighborhood where my mother was teaching; I also attended the junior high school in our neighborhood. I was a good student; my mother was extremely keen to provide a good education for me. She is the one who first helped develop my taste for reading and learning. I had good, loving, and caring teachers in the junior high school. I excelled practically in all subjects. For three consecutive years, I was on the national honor list.

The senior high school turned out to be a bit problematic. There was just one overcrowded high school in Üsküdar, and it had a very bad reputation. My mother was adamant: she would not send me there under any circumstance. She detested that school. But then which one? Under the existing over-regulated central system of public education, she had to register me there, since it was the high school of our district. That did not deter her from having her way. For the first time in her life, she did something illegal. Through an influential friend, she obtained a fake residency certificate that allowed me to register in a public high school with very good credentials that was across from Üsküdar on the other side of the Bosporus.

For me, this was a very welcome decision. Not only was the high school I was going to attend one of the best in Istanbul, but it was also reasonably far from home. Until that time, my schooling had taken place close to home. Now I was going to have some liberty, something that I wanted very much. I was a teenager and motherly supervision was becoming distasteful, to say the least. Attending this school meant that I would take the ferry to cross the Bosporus to the European side and from there take a streetcar to the school, returning home the same way. There were girls on the ferry, on the streetcars. There were no girls in the high school I was going to attend, for it was only for boys, but I could meet a nice girl on the way. The feeling of wanting to be in love was germinating in me. Adolescence was over. I felt like a young man, and, in my mind, a young man had to be in love.

I loved my school. I loved my teachers. To please them was a pleasure for me, especially the mathematics and physics teachers. It was then I decided that I was going to be an engineer. Not only did I like sciences, but I was under the impression that in Turkey, engineers earned lots of money. My mother had a meager salary and we always had money problems. The Second World War was playing havoc with our lives. Prices skyrocketed and there was a shortage of everything. Anything that was any good could be purchased on the black market, but we could ill afford that. I knew the war would not last forever, and as an engineer, I could easily say goodbye to poverty.

My first of three years of senior high school passed rapidly as I intensely studied physics and mathematics, dreaming of becoming rich as an engineer. I was second in my class, and my grades were very good—mostly nines and eights, with the American terminology A minuses and B pluses. Of course, in physics and mathematics I received the top grade of ten. I was the happiest kid on the block. I was dead sure that eventually I was going to be able to enroll in the school of engineering, a very competitive school with a highly difficult entrance exam.

I spent the summer vacation studying mathematics on my own, playing chess with my friends, and occasionally swimming from the shore to Leander's Tower and back. I had not yet found a girlfriend, let alone fallen in love. I kept saying to myself, "next year, definitely." Little did I know that the next year was going to be full of surprises, and bad ones at that.

The next year for me began as any other school year. Good teachers, same classmates, some pretty girls commuting to their schools in the same ferries, and more physics and mathematics. The education system in those years was such that the school year consisted of nine months of studying divided into three trimesters. The grades in each subject were given at the end of each trimester. In order to complete the year, one had to get grades in all subjects that totaled to at least fourteen. If not, one had to take an exam in the failed subject right before the beginning of the next academic year and receive a passing grade, at least above five.

At the end of the first three months, my report card was once again very good, recording mostly tens and just a few nines. The second trimester began after a break of a week. In the meantime, our geography professor lamentably passed away and a new one was appointed as a substitute. I must confess, geography was not a favorite subject of mine. I found it dull, for one had to learn the heights of the mountains, the lengths of the rivers, which country neighbored which one, and so on. Be that as it may, I did well, for I learned those heights and lengths dutifully just as a good student should, and my grade was seven.

The new geography teacher was someone I did not care for. He did not have the warmth like our other teachers, nor did he care much for his students. But I said to myself, "so what?" and continued to give the same attention to the subject. Lo and behold, at the end of the second trimester, my grade in that subject was a miserable three—or translating to the American system, a miserable D minus.

I was flabbergasted. I had no explanation for my failure. I was apprehensive but not alarmed. "It must have been my fault," I said to myself, "maybe I missed the questions." I consoled myself and decided to study a bit harder. At the end of the third trimester I was shocked, for my grade was again three. Since the total of the trimesters was only thirteen, I had failed in geography. My last chance was to repeat the exam after the summer break in order to move to the eleventh grade, the last year of high school. I kept my optimism alive and began memorizing anything and everything that was in the textbook, getting ready for the exam. That summer I did not even turn the first page of my books of mathematics or physics. Geography was coming out of my ears.

However, before the exam I decided to pay a visit to my geography teacher and find out precisely what the reason was for my failure. Perhaps he would suggest that I study more or read other books. He received me at his home rather pleasantly; he even offered a cup of coffee. He told me, unashamedly, that there were two possible solutions for me to obtain a passing grade in the exam. I listened eagerly with the hope that he was going to give me some clues, perhaps to read some other books. How naïve I was!

One possible solution to pass the exam was to bribe him. He demanded 350 liras, ten liras more than my mother's monthly salary. The second solution was, for me, to spend just one hour, not more, in his bedroom with him. He pointed to the door of his bedroom, which was ajar. I could not believe my ears; I could not believe my eyes. A seventeen-year-old lad was going to gratify his teacher sexually? Ever since the first grade, I had been drilled to respect and revere my teachers. They were like holy men, my mother used to say. And now a teacher was making the most disgusting, the most heinous, the most inhuman suggestion, trying to rape his seventeen-year-old student. The whole world began to whirl around me. Even today, I cannot remember how I left his house, how long I sat at the steps of the building, and how I found my way home.

When my mother asked me how the meeting was, I answered her inquiries with a series of lies, saying he had suggested that I should read this or that book, that I should pay greater attention to European geography and a bunch of other stories that I conjured up, despite the fact that we normally didn't tell lies to each other. It had been our unbroken pact until then. I would not have succumbed to any threat to ask from her, a woman who held her profession most sacred, most noble—despite the poor salary—to pay a bribe, even if she had the money, which she did not. But the other "option" was something that I would not dare mention to her or anybody else. If I was to protect her, I had to lie. I continued to study knowing full well that I was doomed.

I failed the exam. I had to repeat the tenth grade. My dreams had crumbled. As a rule, no one can be admitted to the engineering school if he has repeated any grade, and I was to repeat the tenth grade. I was not meant to be an engineer.

I cannot describe the air of grief that descended upon our house. I could not possibly tell anyone why I had failed. My mother could not believe her ears when she heard that I had failed and I had to repeat the tenth grade. My aunt refused to talk to me for a while. My grandmother stated again and again that she wished that she were dead rather than hear such news. Like all bad news, however, its impact faded; the tragic air in the house gradually became less dense, and the urgency of practical solutions began to take precedence.

I was adamant about not continuing in the same high school. My mother was equally adamant that I should not transfer to the neighborhood high school that she originally had rejected. For a few days we were at an impasse. The day came when my mother, who had faced all types of adversities, finally confessed her weakness, and I think for the first time murmured, "I wish your father were alive."

Well, my father was not alive and I had to find a solution to the impasse. To repeat another year in the same school was out of the question. I planned a coup d'état. I went to the school and asked for transfer papers. I stopped being a registered student there. My action had stopped the option of continuing in the same school, but had not brought a viable solution, for my mother did not budge from her position of not transferring me to the neighborhood high school. Quite calmly, but unfalteringly, I put my decision to my mother: either I would quit studying for good and find a job or I would continue my studies in a private high school, knowing that my mother would reject the first option outright. I had already made up my mind which private school I wanted to attend. It was a high school with an impeccable reputation of being the best in Istanbul, and some of the teachers I had in the previous school were also teaching there. But certainly not the geography teacher.

The school was indeed one of the best and the tuition was one of the highest. My mother's salary could not possibly cope with the cost of moving from a tuition-free public high school to a high-tuition private one. The difficulty of the situation was insurmountable at first. I appealed to my aunt, accepting all the blame for the failure. Despite the fact that initially she would not speak to me when she heard I had failed, she had a soft spot for me in her heart. Well, her heart softened further when she saw me with tears in my eyes, and she agreed to help by paying half of the tuition.

For the other half perhaps my uncle, my mother's brother, could help. After all, he was a well-to-do merchant. But all I received was a flat no. He did not even have a penny for me; to him, I was a lazy bum. My last opportunity for assistance came from my mother's cousin, also a rich merchant, who sincerely loved me as a nephew rather than as a cousin and consented to help.

My new school, which I loved from the first day, changed my life and my future and reshaped my aspirations. It was there that I met the best teachers.

The teacher I liked the best taught us philosophy, logic, and sociology. He opened up horizons that I never knew existed. Step by step, he introduced the philosophies of Descartes, Kant, and Hegel, and the power of logical and abstract thinking. Because of him, I realized that there was something wider, deeper, and more gratifying than mathematics, something beyond its well-defined but dry and limited logic. I learned the power of thinking without being a slave to letters and symbols, and soon became aware that logic itself went beyond the boundaries of logical mathematics. Philosophy and logic freed my mind beyond what I thought was possible. I was just like a little boy who suddenly found himself in a toy factory. Like a traveler in the desert who finds an oasis after wandering for many days in the arid wilderness, I furiously gulped the writings of logicians and philosophers.

There was also a wonderful literature teacher at the school. With a great deal of commitment and perseverance, she opened the world of poetry and showed us the beauty of language. Because my one-track mind had been locked onto mathematics and physics, I had neglected reading poetry. Until I became her student, I had been unaware that poetry was also mathematics, but it went beyond anything I had ever learned. Rhymes and meters, sounds and movement of words, describing one's deepest feelings—poetry sparkled with its internal logic and incredible beauty; it was mathematics made in heaven.

Numbers were dull, symbols were philistine, but meters and rhymes were infinitely measured, infinitely noble. The most personal feelings and thoughts of a poet shone among the threads of words, visible to those who understood the thoughts of the writer. Poetry elated the reader who could discover the meanings of the words that lay hidden under the cover of measures of music. To feel and decipher the ambiguity of a poem was, for me, many times more satisfying and gratifying than solving a trigonometric equation. What is more mathematical than music? What is more musical than poetry? Poetry for me was a string of words from which no word could be taken out nor to which a single word could be added without damaging its sound, its inner logic or its meaning, however ambiguous that may be. To hell with physics, to hell with mathematics, to hell with becoming an engineer. The die was cast.

In my new school, I also met the most wonderful, most beautiful girl in the universe. Her blond hair shone like a golden crown, and her green-blue eyes radiated love and care. I knew right then and there that I was in love. For her I was just a friend; for me she was my future wife. I graduated from high school not as the first, but as the second-best student. She was the first. For her entire life, she was bound to remain first in everything. After graduating, she told me that she was going to study economics. Our paths were diverging, for I was determined to study philosophy. We said farewell.

As it turned out, I did not study philosophy because that would have caused a Greek tragedy in our house. What could have been the future of a student of philosophy? At best, a high school teacher. My mother esteemed her profession and taught for miserable pay, but she could not allow her son to be a poorly paid teacher as well. There was no one in the family who agreed with my decision, not even my mother's cousin, whose financial help I needed to be able to attend the university. I cried; my mother cried; and, in the end, I conceded. I was going to join the blue-green-eyed girl and study economics at the same university.

It was in the third year of the university that she fell in love with me. For that to happen, I confess unashamedly, I tried every gimmick and trick—all of them honest, of course. She was my true love; as my wife, she still is.

After graduation, I was appointed to the position of teaching assistant to a professor. Although I had given up philosophy, I had not given up the profession of teaching, a profession that I loved the most. I was burning with the desire to work with young minds and to mold them as my philosophy and literature teachers had done. But I never succeeded doing that in my own country. My studies in philosophy had taken me from Hegel to Marx, the deadliest route one could take in Turkey then.

III

Istanbul, a city in northwest Anatolia and east of Thrace, now has a population of more than fourteen million people. It was first built as the capital of the Eastern Roman Empire in the fourth century by

Constantine the Great and named Constantinople. Over time, the city became the center of splendor and riches throughout Europe. After the collapse of the Roman Empire, it was the capital of the Byzantium Empire until 1453 when the Ottoman Sultan Mehmet II conquered the city, thus ending Byzantium. Constantinople remained the capital of the Ottoman Dynasty until 1923, when the Ottoman Empire came to an end with the disastrous result of the First World War, and the capital was moved to Ankara by the republic.

Nevertheless, Istanbul continues to be the cultural and economic center of the Republic of Turkey. Its unbelievably rich history is displayed in almost every corner by the churches and monuments built by the Greeks and by the mosques, fountains, and palaces of the Ottomans. The Bosporus, which splits the city, runs from north to south and unites the Black Sea with the Marmara Sea, an inlet opening to the Dardanelles, which then connects to the Aegean Sea and the Mediterranean. Two suspended bridges join the two continents of Europe and Asia.

I left my beloved city in March 1953, the city whose every nook and corner I knew well. To me it was the most beautiful city in the world, although at that time I knew no other city in Turkey, except, briefly, Ankara, or anywhere else. My judgment was based simply on my limited experience, not on knowledge of other places. I could not imagine a city more beautiful than Istanbul. It was Eden on Earth.

I remember vividly my grandmother telling me when I was a kid that God had placed two invisible angels on our shoulders. The angel on the left shoulder registered our bad deeds and the one on the right the good ones, and when we went to the other world, the balance between the two would determine whether one went to hell or heaven. For her, hell was where the devils roamed and the sinners burned with flames or were thrown into boiling tar. In contrast, a river ran through heaven, which was full of green hills and mountains and angels playing in an atmosphere of perpetual cool breezes to the sounds of the most beautiful music. Well, Istanbul, with its green hills, blue Bosporus, and cool breezes that came in the hot summer months all the way from the North Pole was the heaven, or paradise, that my grandmother described.

Istanbul's history goes back to time immemorial. Slicing the city into two as if with the brush of a master painter, the Bosporus divides the land into East and West, or Asia and Europe. Nowhere do two worlds, two civilizations, two histories come so close to each other as they do in Istanbul, a city where for more than two millennia these things have lived side by side. When Constantine came with his army in search of a new capital, today's Istanbul was just a forest covering seven hills. Only a small Greek fishing village, Chalcedon, existed at the south entrance of the Bosporus on the Asian side.

Within a few centuries, Constantinople, as it came to be called, was dotted with churches whose altars and walls were adorned with beautiful mosaics. Egyptian obelisks, which were wonders of the world, were erected in the four corners of the city. Impregnable walls protected the city from enemy attacks. There were vineyards in the city. Its huge hippodrome provided a venue for races, festivities, imperial weddings, and sometimes for bloody revolts as well. When the Turks arrived, they adorned the city with mosques, fountains, gardens, palaces, covered bazaars. Istanbul was not only the seat of power, but also the center of art, music, poetry. Looking at Istanbul from a distance, from the Sea of Marmara when the sun sets slowly behind the glittering domes of the mosques, one cannot help but feel the awe of the glory of the centuries.

Santa Sophia, which at one time had the biggest dome in the world, was a Greek church during the Byzantine era that had been turned into a mosque after the conquest and subsequently became a museum with the establishment of the Turkish Republic. This wonderful monument silently narrates the history of Istanbul. Next to it is the seventeenth-century Blue Mosque, with its six minarets visible from every corner of the city because it was built on one of the seven hills, and the Süleymaniye, the mosque built during the reign of Suleiman the Magnificent, with its dome bigger than that of Santa Sophia. Beneath it is Topkapı, the palace of the sultans. Farther along the coast is Dolmabahçe, the new palace built in the mid-nineteenth century of solid marble. All of them were my daily visual feast.

My route to the university always took me through Sultanahmet, the area of the old Greek hippodrome, today a park with two

Egyptian obelisks in its center, adjacent to the Blue Mosque. I had visited all the important mosques and every old church. Some had been turned into mosques; some still remained as churches. The inner walls of many mosques were covered with beautiful tiles designed by the most renowned masters, blue ones, green ones, red ones. Writings by the most ingenious calligraphers hung on both sides of the mosques' altars. I had spent countless hours adoring all of them; they were all known to me.

My Istanbul, the seat of two past empires, is a very malleable city. It meshes and unites very different cultures into a single entity. It is Byzantine, it is Ottoman, it is Turkish, but above all it is Istanbul, with its unique air, sound, and soul.

The Istanbul that I left behind had barely one million inhabitants. Its borders were well defined. The urban sprawl came much later when the population moved from central Anatolia to the big cities, especially to Istanbul, changing irrevocably the character of the city. In those days, its streets were crisscrossed with streetcars. The Bosporus was always adorned with ferries carrying passengers from one side to the other, from its beginning to its end. In its streets lived a Tower of Babel. Turks spoke Turkish, Greeks spoke Greek, Armenians spoke Armenian, and the Jews spoke Ladino, an archaic Spanish dotted with Turkish words. Quite often, French was heard, too.

While the Bosporus divided the city as East and West, the Golden Horn on the European side divided European Istanbul into North and South. The south side was the seat of power during the Ottoman times. At the foot of Santa Sophia is Sarayburnu, or Palace Promontory, the most distinguished geographical landmark of Istanbul. It is also the mark of history, for between it and Santa Sophia stands Topkapı, the living memory of the Ottoman Empire, the empire that had decorated Istanbul with the most beautiful and majestic mosques whose minarets create the illusion of holding up the firmament.

The Topkapı palace is not one single building but a series of kiosks and pavilions ornamented by master calligraphers, painters of miniatures, and abstract designers. One has a breathtaking view of the Bosporus from any one of those buildings. Behind its walls hide beautiful poems with lines more lustrous than a string of pearls, written by Suleiman the Magnificent and Ahmet III, intricate melodies composed by Selim III, as well as the glories, intrigues, opulence, riots, and assassinations, and the ghosts of the most gorgeous women of the entire empire, eunuchs, servants, men of sword, and men of pen. Topkapı is not the set of a second-rate robbery film as depicted on the silver screen with the same title. It contains the entire Ottoman history with all its glory and decadence.

The north side was much more cosmopolitan. In Byzantine times, the Genovese and their traders took over the north shore of the Golden Horn. In the Ottoman times, the "Frenks"—that is, the Europeans—were there, and there they built their embassies, their houses, and their businesses. Pious Turks called the north side Giaour Istanbul, Istanbul of the Infidels. Naturally, after the establishment of the republic, all embassies moved to Ankara, but their majestic buildings remain as consulates. Most of the movie houses were on the north side, as were the luxurious restaurants, bars, and coffee houses with French names like Le Bon, Marquise, Degustation. There were foreign language bookshops like Hachette, selling books in French, and Buchhaus, for German literature. There was even a bookshop called Holy Books that sold the Old and the New Testament in all the known languages. Neither Hachette nor Buchhaus are there anymore. One is a Starbucks, and the other is a MacDonald's.

The Bosporus could only be God's own creation. A zigzag course of water flowing between undulating hills covered with trees green in the summer and green, yellow, and red trees in the fall. It snowed a lot in the winter. The entire city was white; the hills, too. Only the pine trees on the hills remained green, green and white.

In early spring, a white, clean fog would descend upon the Bosporus. The hills would be hidden behind a misty curtain and the city would become an unknown land of dreams. The only reality was the horns of the ferry boats navigating on the Bosporus. Some horns were deep and bass, some had the voice of a soprano who had a cold. The horns always tooted short and always just once, waiting for a response from the traffic on the opposite side.

From hundreds of minarets, the city would awaken with the ezan, the muezzin's call to the faithful to come to prayers. Those who resided in the vicinity of the churches woke up with the bells that rang daily at six o'clock.

IV

Üsküdar, the district where I was born, was founded in the seventh century BC by the inhabitants of the Greek colony of Chalcedon and was called Chrysopolis, perhaps because it was a wealthy little port. In medieval times, the name was changed to Scutari and then to Üsküdar. It is Istanbul's oldest residential district, with a more relaxed atmosphere. It is directly opposite the old city and the Leander's tower, which was built on a tiny islet at the entrance of Istanbul harbor.

According to legend, one of the Byzantine emperors had a beautiful daughter whom he loved dearly. The soothsayers forecast that the girl was going to be bitten by a snake one day and die. To protect his daughter, the emperor had the tower built, named it after his daughter, Leander, and had her live there. But keeping her in the tower could not stop what was foretold from happening. She was bitten by a snake that had crawled into the basket of flowers carried by her lover and died. The tower is known today as Kızkulesi, Maiden's Tower. It is one of the city's symbols.

Üsküdar is home to many historical mosques and Ottoman buildings. It is also home to several religious monuments, including the tomb of Aziz Mahmut, who was the founder of the Halveti Sufi order, as well as the tomb of Nasuhi Efendi, who was the founder of another Sufi order. Üsküdar has an air of mysticism. It became famous during the Crimean War as the location of the British army hospital in which Florence Nightingale served as a nurse. Five kilometers east of the city center is the famous hill of Çamlıca, the highest point in Istanbul that commands the panoramic view of the entire city and the four beautiful islands at the south entrance of the Bosporus. These islands were used for exile in Byzantine times and are now the center of aquatic sports and the playground of the rich. South of Üsküdar is Kadıköy, the old Chalcedon, which includes fashionable residential areas, such as Moda and Suadiye.

Üsküdar, this modest suburb of Istanbul, is on the Asian side of the Bosporus. I never liked Üsküdar very much. When I was growing up, it was a sleepy district where people of lower income usually resided, as they still do. Its narrow, winding cobblestone streets and old wooden houses with their gardens are relics from the previous century. I remember how, as the sun began to set, the street vendors made their rounds in the neighborhoods. First the milkman would begin to advertise his products. His milk was fresh and his yogurt was creamy. Invariably, the next vendor was the pickle seller. His cabbage, cucumber, and eggplant pickles were famous and a feast for the palate, according to him, anyway. The third and the last peripatetic vendor marketed his boza, a drink made of fermented bread and millet, an elixir for the old and the young.

When it became dark, lights appeared one by one behind the thin curtains of the windows, and as soon as the müezzin invited the believers from the minarets to the last prayer of the night, Üsküdar buried itself in the silence of sleep. The streets became empty, save for a few gaslights' flickering flames that lit the major streets.

Üsküdar's only fame was the view of the European panorama of the city. Standing on its sea coast, one could admire from afar Istanbul's splendor, its palaces, the Ottoman Empire's Topkapı palace, the Dolmabahçe palace dating back to the age of Tanzimat, known to the Europeans as the age of grand Ottoman reform of the nineteenth century, and the European imitation of the Beyoğlu district. The golden glimmer of the sunset, which lasts only a few minutes on the window panes of the houses along its coast as seen from the European side, gave inspiration to a few poets. "It lasts but only a few moments / The glory of poor Üsküdar," wrote Yahya Kemal, one of them. Every resident of Üsküdar had one strong but unfulfilled desire: to move to Kadıköy or to buy a flat in Beyoğlu, north of the Golden Horn, however small it might be. Only a few residents of means could perhaps think of moving to Moda or to Suadiye, fashionable suburbs of Istanbul on the Asian side.

On one of my nostalgic trips I once again took the fifteen-minute trip from the city's harbor in Europe to Üsküdar in Asia. The trip offers a quick glimpse of the Princes' Islands at the entrance of the Bosporus, where the Byzantine emperors kept their enemies after blinding them, and Leander's Tower. When I landed, I found the ferry station very different from what it had been when I left Üsküdar many years earlier. It had changed completely.

I walked along the avenue of Hâkimiyet-i Milliye, the principal thoroughfare that leads to the hill toward Doğancılar. There was not the slightest resemblance between the Üsküdar of my memories and the Üsküdar I saw. If I had not seen the three major mosques where I had prayed many times as a young man, I could honestly swear that I was in a town where I had never been before.

I looked around the square adjacent to the ferry station and searched for the streetcars painted in two colors: the first class in red, the second in green. They had disappeared, and with them the steel rails that used to shimmer in the sunlight. I knew that they had ceased to exist, but I still yearned to see them. Nor was there the kiosk where the vendor sold the newspapers, shouting their names to his patrons who used to come off the boat. He knew them personally and gave them their customary newspaper before they asked for it.

Gone were the car ferries with two paddles on their right and left, which left every two hours for Kabataş across on the European coast, puffing their black smoke from their stacks; gone as well was the station from where they left. In its stead were fishmongers selling their fish, claiming loudly they could not be any fresher. Next to the fishermen were the street vendors, with big old towels wrapped around their waists, selling köftes, Turkish-style hamburgers, from carts mounted on three discarded bicycle wheels. They claimed the burgers were worth tasting, placing them in a halved quarter loaf of bread with fresh tomatoes and hot peppers and calling out, "get your hot, hot köftes."

When we were young, going to the square, which harbored the ferry station, and looking for the girls with whom we thought we were in love, was a big part of our lives. We pretended that we were waiting for our acquaintances or neighbors coming off the ferry returning to their homes. We were actually there to watch the girls who secretly watched us from the corner of their eyes as they came off the ferry. But now, neither the young men were there, nor were the girls coming off the ferry. Obviously the secret intimate meeting places had changed. I continued to walk.

All the shops I had known were gone, torn down, razed. Neither the Bulgarian dairy shop nor Andon's butcher shop was there. They had been the centerpiece of luxury for Üsküdar. Andon was famous for selling the best meat. His prices were a bit higher than other butchers'. He was the first butcher to keep a refrigerator in his shop. In the shop window during the day, he displayed animal carcasses stamped in mauve ink either as lamb or mutton, hanging them by their legs with an iron hook; at night, when he closed his shop at seven o'clock, he kept them in the refrigerator. People hurried to catch the ferry that left the European side at six-fifteen in the evening, fearing that Andon would close his shop and they would not be able to make it there in time. He always maintained that he was of Greek origin; to us, he was a Christian Albanian. He spoke in Albanian with his son. I wonder why he claimed that he was Greek when there was not much sympathy for the Greeks but the Albanians were well-respected. Could it be that he thought that street urchins would follow him and shout insulting phrases like "Zoti Albanian, his bottom is vermilion?"

The Bulgarian's dairy was next to Andon's shop. Two brothers worked there. All the residents of Üsküdar knew them personally, but only those who were relatively well-to-do bought their milk, yoghurt, and butter there. They swore that theirs was the best, the cleanest, and the tastiest merchandise. It was a well-established belief that Bulgarians were the best dairymen—that is, until the war started and prices of everything went sky-high. All of a sudden, the municipality closed the dairy shop for a week, claiming that the brothers adulterated the butter, and subjected them to a fine. The customers were divided in their opinion. Some argued that it was discrimination against Christians and that the municipal police had tricked them because they had refused to pay the usual bribe; others argued that the taste of the butter they sold had changed lately and the Bulgarians were indeed guilty of adultery. Now, in the place of these two shops stood buses using diesel oil, polluting the air with the black smoke spewing from their exhaust pipes.

The grocery store that was quite close to the dairy and the butcher had also gone. It sold all that was necessary for the kitchen. At the entrance, there were big sacks of dry beans, chick peas, red and green lentils, powdered sugar, and rice. Inside, white cheese swam in big tin cans. The shop window displayed dry pastrami, sausages, and a huge wheel of cheese similar to the Italian caciocavallo. On the shelves were bars of soap and bottles of olive oil. On the floor stood a barrel of cured black olives. And at the back was the owner himself, beside him his apprentice, whose main function was to swat away the flies with a fly swatter. The swatter was nothing more than a simple tool made from a stick with one centimeter-wide strips of paper of different colors tied at one end. It did not kill the flies, just shooed them away and prevented them from settling on the merchandise. The apprentice swayed that stick with great pride and always kept his eyes on the flies, even while he handed the required merchandise and paper bags to his master. Now a big market occupies the site where the small grocery store stood. Its door was closed when I walked by. I looked in through its windows. It was full of packaged stuff. The apprentice with the fly swatter was not there anymore. The flies were outside and looking in, just like me.

I continued to walk. I wondered what had happened to the patisserie that used to be on the right-hand side and the candy shop across the street from it. During the eve of the religious festivities, people lined up at its door; the candy that is traditionally distributed to the attendants of a special rite held in a mosque forty days after the death of an individual was sold there in paper cones. The best red-colored sugar from which a drink was made and offered after childbirth could be found there, as well. Children bought the coconut-flavored white candy with a marking of a lion on one side and displayed in glass jars, and the banana-flavored candy that melted like butter in one's mouth. The patisserie had white marble-topped tables and leather upholstered chairs around them. In its window were displayed a variety of tortes, tarts, cakes, baklava, and half a dozen other desserts that are the pride of Ottoman-Turkish cuisine. During the summer months, a paper sheet placed on the glass listed the kinds of ice cream that were available, inviting people to come in and savor them. Neither the patisserie nor the candy shop was there any longer. The site had been taken over by two shops—one was selling household appliances, and the other sold tapes, radios, televisions, computers, and electronic equipment.

I reached the bottom of the hill that would take me to Doğancılar. Right there used to be the only movie house, Hâle, meaning "halo." It was there that we watched cheap Egyptian films with the actors singing songs, shaking the tassels of their fezzes from one side to the other, or the entire adventures of Dick Tracy. It had now become Cinerama.

There was no resemblance between the Üsküdar of my memories and the Üsküdar I was in now. Though I had never liked the neighborhood I grew up in, I was very sad not to have found it intact. Why, I do not know. Üsküdar had changed as everything else had changed, probably for the better.

I hailed a cab. The driver invited me in and asked, "Where to?"

For no reason at all I said, "To Kadıköy."

He honked loudly and rushed with great speed toward the road to Kadıköy. He was a youngish man from the northeast corner of Turkey. I could tell because he pronounced the letter "k" as "ch." He asked me whether I was from Kadıköy, the old Chalcedon.

So as not to enter into a conversation I curtly said, "Yes."

As if he was talking to himself he said, "Kadıköy is a wonderful place, isn't it? Hopefully we, too, will be living there pretty soon." He banged on the steering wheel of the car and continued, "I have two more installments to pay for this car; thereafter, God willing, I will be moving to Kadıköy. What do you say? Üsküdar is not a livable place, is it?"

Well, I had lived there for twenty-two years.

4
Childhood Memories

I

Childhood memories, some sad, some incredibly sweet, and others completely baffling, linger until one's dying day. To relate all of it is bound to be boring. Some memories begin to fade as one grows older. Four of my own, however, have remained quite vivid in my mind. They are the ones related here.

An early memory is that of my circumcision, a memory that has mystified me all through my life. Circumcision, a ritual that is prepared meticulously with a great deal of pride, is an unforgettable childhood memory for any Turkish man. It is a mysterious religious and festive rite to which every seven-year-old boy is readied many days in advance. The first item to prepare is a new suit adorned with a sash that extends down diagonally from the right shoulder, crossing over the heart and ending at the left hip. It should be of red and white silk ribbon or sash, representing the colors of the flag. It is attached to the shoulder of the jacket with a fancy pin that has a large blue bead on which the word mashallah—may God avert the evil eye—is written in Arabic letters. The blue stone is meant to ward off the evil eye.

The proud parents take their son, clad in his new suit with the sash, to visit aunts and uncles, all other immediate members of the family, distant relatives, and, of course, the neighbors. The boy is the center of attention for about a month. He kisses the hands of the elders, and, in turn, the elders kiss him. He receives gifts of chocolates, candy, money, a beautiful embroidered handkerchief, and sometimes even a gold coin. Everyone wishes him good luck.

He is told that this rite of passage will make him clean and that he will be a real Muslim. So much attention leaves him in a daze; he senses that something wonderful will happen to him, but, in an almost fairy tale atmosphere, he is not quite sure what—until one afternoon, the circumciser, with a swift hand movement and a great deal of dexterity, cuts off his foreskin. A sharp pain makes him shriek with pain, and then the festivities start. Every person whose hand he kissed is invited to the celebration. A clown tries to entertain him and he tries to forget his pain. Food and drinks are served and, as the custom dictates, all invitees shower the child with gifts, mostly toys, books, watches, and cameras. It is a proud moment in the life of the parents. Grownups enjoy themselves and the boy cries with pain, on and off.

Like all Turkish boys, I, too, went through the same ritual when I was seven, two months before I started grade school. My father took me to his tailor and had a dark blue suit made for me with short trousers and a jacket with gold plated buttons embossed with tiny anchors. He also bought me a pair of black patent leather shoes and white socks. My grandmother, a dressmaker, made an ivory-colored silk shirt for me.

I did not know what circumcision meant. I had no idea that a piece of my body, however insignificant it might be, was going to be separated from me permanently. I had no friends in the neighborhood who had gone through the same experience. All I knew was what was told to me, that I would be clean forever and become a real Muslim. Day after day, I visited my relatives in my new suit. I became spoiled well beyond the level at which I was already spoiled, for I was the only child at home; all attention was always on me anyway.

Two or three days before the appointed day of the circumcision, my grandmother said, "Get dressed—we are going to the mausoleum of Aziz Mahmut Efendi to pray."

He was a well-known aziz, meaning saint, of Üsküdar, who made people's wishes come true, cured the sick, and eased their pain. My grandmother truly believed in him. Not that I knew much how to pray, but I was eager to go to the mausoleum and ask him to make me a clean and good and proud Muslim.

Along with my mother, we left home early in the morning, for the mausoleum was quite far from where we lived. We walked down the hill from our house, passed the market, crossed the only avenue of Üsküdar, climbed another hill with a street paved with uneven cobblestones, and entered a narrow and winding dirt road that ended in a cul-de-sac. On both sides of the road were old, dilapidated wooden houses.

At the end of the road stood a small mosque. Next to it was a very small one-story building, almost a shack, which was the mausoleum of the saint. It had two windows at the street level barred with iron rods. Looking through one of the windows, I remember seeing four biers, two big and two small, covered with green silk velvet and embroidered with quotations from the Koran in gold and silver threads.

Standing in front of the windows, my grandmother raised her hands with palms turned upward and began to murmur. She prayed, but I did not know what she said. In the middle of her prayer she turned her head, looked at me lovingly, and simply said, almost whispering, "Pray, son, pray."

I imitated her, opened my hands as she had done, extended my arms and started to pray. I don't remember what I mumbled. I guess I asked the saint to help me become a good Muslim and be a clean boy. My mother stayed a few steps behind us. She was not really a believer, but she was not about to object to her mother; in fact, she never dreamed of objecting. Old-style education reigned in our home. I shall never forget what happened after that.

We were about to finish our prayer and leave when a man appeared out of nowhere. Him, I remember well. He was a tall man, maybe about forty years old, wearing an impeccable dark blue suit. He had a grey hat and a walking stick in his hand. "So," he said with a sweet voice, "the little one is getting ready to be circumcised, eh?" He ruffled my hair and patted my cheek.

My mother, who was not observant as I said and did not actually care for praying, wanted to cut the encounter short. "Yes, Sir, we just finished our prayers and we are going back home."

With the same sweet voice the man said, "Sister, would you like to enter inside and pray once more?"

My mother did not quite know how to answer. Clearly she was not in favor of entering the mausoleum. She might have been even afraid. It was the tenth year of the republic, the Atatürk era, and with the desire to take Turkey onto the road of secularism, the government had banned and closed all religious institutions; mausoleums of the saints were under lock and key; the dervish orders were banned; and all overtly religious manifestations were declared illegal. Being a schoolteacher and a real believer of Atatürk's principles, my mother, obviously, did not want to enter the mausoleum.

The man in the dark blue suit took a key with a gold chain attached from his vest pocket. "Come on," he said, "I am the attendant of the mausoleum. Let the young one pray inside just for a moment."

He put the key into the padlock that was hanging on the door and we went in. It was indeed a small room, barren and spotlessly clean. I remember a faint musty smell.

Two days later I found out what to be a clean and real Muslim meant. I am told that today anesthesia is used in the surgery, but in those days no such thing existed. I cried my heart out, though not for long, when a piece of skin was removed permanently from my body. The sharp pain subsided fairly quickly and the toys were wonderful.

I think it was two or perhaps three weeks later my grandmother said, "Now that you can wear your trousers, let us go, son, and give our thanks to Aziz Mahmut Efendi."

And so we did. This time my mother did not join us. Down the hill, then up the next hill we went again, to the narrow winding street, the mosque and the mausoleum of the saint. As expected, the door was padlocked.

We approached the window. My grandmother prayed and I imitated her and said,

"Let's go, Grandma, I finished my prayer."

I was in a hurry to leave, for she had promised to buy me a bar of chocolate at the market on the way back, and chocolate was my favorite sweet. It still is.

"Let us see," she said, "let us see whether we can find that fine gentleman, the mausoleum attendant. Maybe he will come by and we can enter inside and pray once more."

We stood and waited for a while, but no one came by and no one was in the street. My grandmother almost gave up when a woman appeared at the other end of the street. When she came quite near us my grandmother greeted her by bidding her a good morning and asked, "Good sister, where can we find the attendant of the mausoleum? Do you know?"

Flabbergasted, the woman looked at my grandmother for a moment and whispered, "There is no attendant of the mausoleum. There has not been one for years. Don't you know, sister, Atatürk closed all the mausoleums. We are secular now. Don't look for trouble, go home now, don't dilly dally, just go before you get into trouble, go."

And she walked away with quick steps. I remember looking back at the door of the mausoleum. A rusty padlock and rusty chains were still dangling on the door.

It certainly was not a dream. Nor was it a fanciful thought. The man in the dark blue suit had been there with his grey hat and walking stick. He had the key on a gold chain. He had opened the door. I will never forget him. He is more vivid in my mind than my circumcision ceremony, but I guess I will never know who he was.

II

My second childhood memory is one of remorse, a feeling I can't rid myself of even after so many decades. Remorse is a moral suffering caused by knowing that one has acted badly and incorrectly. It is a bitter suffering, the heart's torture after a guilty action. It is more bitter than repentance, which designates a spiritual sadness with a religious undertone. Remorse is a torture, an anxiety and punishment, while repentance is a virtue. Remorse is quite different from regret, which one feels after committing a voluntary act and does not necessarily imply a moral blame. It is an ethical regret, which may very well be permanent, which has been the case with me.

The year was 1935. I was eight years old and a student in the second grade of primary school. The new neighborhood to which we moved in Üsküdar consisted mostly of lower- and middle-class working families, far away from the glittering lights, busy traffic, and affluence of the city center on the European side. There also lived some well-to-do families, but they were too few and far between. It was a somber and conservative neighborhood known as Sultantepe, the Sultan's Hill.

No one knew exactly why it was called the Sultan's Hill. I believe it was so named because it commanded an absolutely majestic and extraordinarily beautiful view of the Bosporus as it opened to the Marmara Sea and reached almost halfway to the north, where the Ottoman Turks had built their fortifications to put an end to the Byzantine Empire in the fifteenth century. Huge boats, mostly cargo ships, and oil tankers flying flags from Russia, Bulgaria, Romania, England, France, and other countries frequently crossed the deep blue waters of this narrow passage between Europe and Asia. Local ferries carried passengers, some following the western shore and some the eastern, stopping at the ferry stations of the villages located on its coast, while other ferries carried passengers a short distance from the Asian to the European side and back.

From the hill, one had a view of Istanbul proper, of the palaces on its shores, thick wooded hills in the background with pine trees, elms, poplars, oaks, and Judas trees, their purple flowers heralding the arrival of spring. Sitting on the edge of the hill and watching the Bosporus on sunny summer days was the main pastime for children and grownups alike. The sunset behind the trees was a sight to behold. The last rays painted the windows of Sultantepe's houses first yellow and then flaming crimson for a minute or two. And then the müezzins from the minarets called the faithful to prayer. It was time to return home. About the same time, men returned from work with a loaf of bread under their arms. The whole neighborhood was ready for the silence of the night.

No house in the neighborhood had a radio; television had not been invented yet. In the spring, kids flew kites and grownups gossiped while sitting on the ridge. In the hot summer months, people watched the Bosporus and tried to cool off whenever the north breeze rustled the leaves of the ancient trees. Children counted the boats that went by or played hide-and-seek or catch-me-if-you-can. In the winter, most families huddled in a single room where there was one stove for heating and cooking. When night fell, curtains were drawn and darkness covered the neighborhood, save for the glow that came from sparsely located gas lamps in the streets, shedding their faint yellow light on the rough cobblestones.

We lived on what I used to think of as a downhill street. In any case, most of Sultantepe's streets were downhill—or uphill, if you like. Wooden houses lined both sides of our street. Most were two-story structures, and many were covered with very old, dirty, ochre-colored planks, bent and curled from the heat of the summer months. Some houses were patched with used kerosene cans, the easiest and cheapest way of repair, for wood was very expensive.

Our house was at the top of the street, close to the ridge of the hill. It was slightly inclined to the left, and some of its broken windows were patched with cardboard to be replaced with glass whenever extra funds were available, not easy for a poorly paid grade school teacher. Farther downhill from our house was a decrepit old house with a big garden that had some fruit trees. An elderly couple lived there. The husband was an Albanian. Rumors had it that he was one of the gardeners in the palace of King Ahmed Zog. In 1939, the king literally sold his country for a handful of gold to Mussolini who was dreaming of building a colonial empire. The Italian army walked into Tirana without firing a shot. My elderly neighbor did not want to live under the occupation of "infidel Christians," for he was devout, and thus opted for exile. Luckily, his wife was of Turkish origin. She had become an orphan at the age of five and had been adopted by a rich family, also of Turkish origin, which had settled in Tirana ages ago. But adoption in those days, in more cases than not, was akin to servitude. It meant to just exist, eat, sleep, and do all the household chores. Those who were adopted had no family rights, no voice within the family; they simply existed. The accepted rule was to have them married as soon as possible and see the last of them.

The lowly gardener had married that "adopted girl" when she was fifteen and he well in his forties. She must have been a beautiful girl in her teens, for even in her old age she was still a good-looking woman: tall and erect, with dark blue eyes and snow-white hair. She always covered her head with a spotless white muslin scarf, not for religious reasons, for half of her hair was visible, but out of habit. She spoke with a typical Balkan Turkish accent, a sing song, tilting her head left and right as she spoke.

When the time came to leave Tirana, the most logical country to go to was Turkey. The rich family showed its last "generosity" to their adopted daughter. They had properties in Istanbul, among them the house in our neighborhood, which was unoccupied, and the couple was told that they could live there as long as the Italian occupation continued. The penniless couple took refuge in that decrepit house with the big garden full of fruit trees.

I do not know how they managed to survive; it was a mystery. I only know that this couple was the poorest of the poor on our street and survived only by the generosity of those less poor than they. I suspect they ate meat once a year during the religious feast that comes seventy days after the end of Ramadan, when a sheep is usually sacrificed and its meat distributed among the poor. Some of the more fortunate in our neighborhood also sacrificed a sheep and distributed its meat among the poor. The gardener and his wife usually received some big chunks.

Winter was a harsh period for those who did not have enough money to buy firewood. The gardener and his wife could not spare any money for heating. In the winter months, the wife visited the neighbors frequently who at least had one heated room. Sometimes she came to our house to warm up her aching bones. We loved her very much, for she would tell stories to entertain us. Sometimes it was the fairy tale about a sultan and his beautiful daughter who fell in love with a prince who in fact was a jinni, and sometimes she told us the story of Muhammad's son-in law, Ali, who cut off the heads of one hundred infidels with one swing of his sword. She rarely spoke about Tirana. Whenever she did, she told the story of the king, his beautiful palace, his procession through the streets of the capital on horseback, and his courageous deeds. The children just loved to listen to her. The parents showed their gratitude by giving her some leftovers.

In the summer months, like everybody else, she was also at the ridge of the hill with all the neighbors on our street, to get a bit of fresh air and to hear a bit of gossip. After 1939, the majority of the conversations were about the war. Whether Germans were going to attack Turkey, why prices were going up so high, which goods were going to be rationed next after bread, tea, coffee, and sugar. Those days were not happy days. The cost of every item in the market soared; many goods simply disappeared from the shelves of shops and became obtainable only in the black market at outrageous prices. The poor neighborhood became poorer by the day. The joy, whatever there had been of it before, was completely gone.

The husband never accompanied his wife to the hill. She always had excuses for him. He was reading the Koran at home, his legs were aching, and so on. Actually, I think the poor gardener had never really learned Turkish. He would have felt out of place. I guess he wanted to be alone with his loneliness. He was a very old and very thin small man with beady, sunken eyes. He had a white pointed beard, shaven head, and tiny hands. We saw him only in the summer months when he sat in a low chair by the door of their house with a couple of baskets next to him containing the fruits he collected from their garden—plums, pears, apricots, cherries. They didn't look very appetizing; nonetheless, the old man always tried to entice the passerby to buy some of them. His voice was soft with a tinge of begging. He pointed to the baskets and begged with his thick Albanian accent, "Please buy, my lady, please buy."

With his limited Turkish, he mostly mispronounced the names of the fruits he sold. In his hand he always had a gadget that he had manufactured himself. It was a long stick with a bunch of thinly cut papers attached to it with a string. He frequently swung the stick over the fruits to shoo the flies off, those unwelcome companions of the whole neighborhood in the summer months. I never saw anybody buy anything from him, and yet, very persistently, he sat next to his baskets from sunrise to sundown.

During the summer months, my mother and I used to go to the market for our daily food shopping. We walked two miles to the market and two miles back. It was not a pleasant trip on hot summer days; the sun would emit its hot rays fairly early in the morning. We did not have a fridge—in fact, nobody in the neighborhood had a fridge. All we knew was that a fridge was an ice making box in which food was preserved. We all knew about it, but no one in the neighborhood had seen one. So in the summer months to go to the market and buy the daily food items, and sometimes a block of ice, was an inescapable chore. On our way, I saw the old man sitting in front of his house trying to sell the fruits of his garden. I felt great pity for him; his soft, begging, melancholy voice was very penetrating. It is still in my ears.

Several times I tried to convince my mother to buy something from him, knowing that she could not spend her limited amount of money frivolously, as she had enough only for our most urgent necessities. So she always answered: "For the same amount of money we can buy better quality items in the market." No doubt she was right, for she had no other choice—she had to stretch every penny to provide for me and for my grandmother. My mother was the only breadwinner, earning a meager salary as a grade school teacher.

My mother gave me a weekly allowance that was barely enough to buy my favorite weekly magazine and two bars of chocolate. Several times I made myself a promise of saving the money I spent on chocolate for a week or two and then buy some fruit from the old man, maybe two pears or a handful of plums. But a ten-year-old boy has little willpower. Invariably I succumbed to the sweet taste of chocolate wrapped in shiny paper and never bought anything from the old man. I do not think anybody bought any fruit from him, although every night before I slept I prayed to God that he would sell some the next day. It was a simple prayer that my grandmother taught me which was called Amentü, I believe. It went something like this: "I believe in God, his prophets, his angels, his books, and the day of judgment." And I always added, "Please, God, let the old man sell something tomorrow, please."

I guess God never heeded my prayers. I believe it was the third year of our move to the house in Sultantepe that we heard the old man had died. Then, and only then, I felt angry with myself. I felt angry, for I had not saved a few pennies to buy some fruit from him. I had not responded even once to his soft, begging voice, nor had I given him the satisfaction of selling something.

Those days are gone now, and despite our relative poverty then, I have only sweet memories of my childhood in Sultantepe. Only sweet memories and the one single remorse, which still lingers; it will haunt me until my dying day, and the silhouette of his face will linger with me forever.

A long time has passed since those days, more than half a century. Once in a while I dream of him. I dream that I am walking alone and I have a handful of coins in my palm. I am buying fruit from him. His face is not old, but radiant and happy. He says a few words that I do not understand. I imagine that is probably what Albanian sounds like. It is a weird dream, for the red, green, and yellow fruits I buy have unusual shapes. I know they are fruit, but

I do not know what kind. I have never seen them before. Then I wake up and for a split second I feel extremely happy that it was only a dream. But soon my remorse returns to haunt me.

III

The third childhood memory is perhaps my sweetest, of which I feel very proud, prouder than graduating from grade school as the first in my class.

It was a national festival day. Festive days or holidays abound in Turkey. There are two religious holidays every year. One celebrates the end of the fasting days of Ramadan, and the other comes forty days after that. Both are full of joy, the rekindling of religious and spiritual feelings. There are also national holidays, the most important of which is the Republic Day. The country adorns itself in the red and white colors of Turkey, practically every city holds military parades, the country's leaders congratulate the people, and speeches are given reaffirming the nation's independence and belief in the republic. Another national holiday is May 19, the day that Atatürk set foot on the Anatolian soil to begin the fight against the occupying forces. Yet another national holiday is celebrated on August 30, the date of the decisive victory against the Greek army that had occupied a large chunk of Western Anatolia.

For children, perhaps the most important holiday was the April 23 celebration. That was the day on which the Grand National Assembly of the revolutionary government met for the first time in Ankara in 1921. It is also known as the Children's Festivity Day. All the children gather on specific avenues where parades are held and flags fly from the buildings. On that day, children are treated like grownups and feel like grownups.

The event I relate here occurred when I was in the last year of grade school. The fourth- and fifth-year students of all elementary schools in Üsküdar were to gather in front of the building of the Popular Republican Party, which was then the only legal political entity. Speeches were going to be given, and military bands were going to play patriotic tunes. But what was most important for us was that only one student would be selected from the fifth grade of every elementary school in Üsküdar, and each child selected was expected to give a speech not lasting more than five minutes.

Our teacher had explained the process to us in the classroom. The delicate question was: which student was going to represent our school? To make the choice as impartial as possible, our teacher proposed the following: we were all going to write a composition on the importance of the day. From among them, she would select the five best and read them in class without revealing the name of the writer. Then the class would vote for the best and the author of that essay would give the speech.

Well, we all took our papers and pencils and started to write. But there was a problem. My mother was a teacher in the same school. Although she was not the teacher of the fifth grade that year, there could be rumors of nepotism if I was selected. In fact, there were cases when some schoolmates who were particularly naughty escaped punishment, but if I did half of what they had done, I would have been penalized just so that nobody could say, "he is the son of a teacher, hence he gets special treatment."

The bell rang; the lesson hour was over, and the teacher collected the papers. We anxiously awaited the results that would be announced the next day. Some of us, I know, prayed; others lit candles at the sacred tombs in the neighborhood; yet others gave all their daily allowances to the poor as alms. None of us wanted to take the chance of losing the opportunity of standing on the balcony of the building of the Republican National Party and speaking, even if it was only for five minutes.

The next day, our teacher entered the classroom with a batch of papers in her hand. We were all ears. I was quite certain that my composition would be one of the five selected, for I had done my best. In fact, the second one she read was mine. I was as happy as a lark, but I could not show it, for she had forewarned us not to show our emotions; or she would discard the composition. You cannot imagine how much we loved our teacher and how much we feared her.

The classroom was totally silent. The selected compositions were read. Our teacher said: "Pick up a small piece of paper and write which one you liked best ranking them from one to five." All of us voted. Of course, I voted unashamedly for mine as the best. I am sure the other four nominees must have done the same.

To keep the story short, I won. I was so excited I did not know what to do. Right in the classroom I wanted to jump up and down with joy, which, of course, was not permissible. I could hardly wait for the bell to ring announcing the end of the class hour. As soon as the school day was over I told everyone I knew that I had won the competition, that I was the first. I was going to be one of the speakers. That for me was the greatest honor.

From the evening of that day until the morning of April 23, I went out into our garden to learn by heart the composition I had written, articulating in a loud voice and moving my hands and arms the way I would when I recited it. I had given up doing homework and was going around in the neighborhood telling all the kids that I was the one who was going to give the speech on April 23.

The day arrived. All the students of the fourth and fifth year gathered in the schoolyard. Boys were dressed in their best suits and girls in their best dresses. The flag bearer led the way, followed by the principal; all the other teachers followed him. The procession began to walk toward the specified building where the ceremony was to take place, singing all the marches we knew, including the one celebrating the tenth anniversary of the establishment of the Turkish Republic. Since our school was located on a hill, we walked down through narrow cobblestone streets to join the others.

We approached the Party building. It was the most beautiful building in the neighborhood and was decked out with flags—the national flag and the Party's flag with the six arrows representing its principles of etatism, nationalism, laicism, populism, revolutionism, and republicanism. A band played in front of the building. The ceremony began, and we sang the national anthem. First the head of the district spoke, then the Party leader. I do not remember who else spoke. Then the students representing the schools were called in. The head of the education office of the district organized us according to the number assigned to the schools. My school was number twenty-four, which meant I was going to be the last speaker. My heart was throbbing and I was in no mood to listen to the speakers before me. I was blocking my ears with my hands and repeating my speech in my head over and over again.

My turn came. I stood on the balcony and told the audience how important April 23 was for the children of today and tomorrow and that we were always ready to serve our fatherland and that the hearts of the children beat for that purpose. My speech lasted five minutes and I finished it with these words: "Our father

Atatürk, I address you" —he was still alive then—"we, today's children will always protect and defend the republic that you have entrusted us."

You cannot imagine the applause I received. I left the balcony. The party leader shook my hand as if I were an adult, ruffled my hair, and congratulated me with the words, "You did well, my son. If you work hard enough you will become a good orator." I don't know whether I walked or flew down the stairs, for I was dying to tell my mother and my teacher what the Party leader told me.

As I left the building I stopped and thought. Suppose they don't believe me when I tell them what he said? My mother would get suspicious right away. She had a reason for that. She knew that I exaggerated and mixed up what happened with what could have happened. She used to get extremely angry when I did that, saying, "Son, don't make up things. Tell them straightforward without exaggeration, without imagining." When I did not follow her advice, she scolded me severely and withheld my weekly allowance of chocolate.

I remember one incident when that occurred. I had finished the first year of grade school. That summer we were vacationing in Bostancı, a seaside district of Istanbul. My mother took me to a tea garden one day. It was not very crowded. I had found a stick and tied a rope to the end of it, using it as a horse. As I was running around in the garden, two ladies who were sitting at another table called me and asked me what my name was, which grade I was in, where I lived, and so on. One of the ladies wanted to know the profession of my father. I could have told her that he had gotten sick and died, but I could not bring myself to tell the truth. On the spot, I made up a story that he was a naval officer, that the boat he was on capsized in a storm on the Black Sea and that one by one he saved the lives of four crew members, and as he returned to save the fifth, he had drowned. The poor ladies were so sorry to hear this tragic tale that they got up from their chairs and approached my mother, to console her, I suppose. I continued with my game. I distinctly remember the kind of scolding I received on the way back home. But one does not give up one's habits, does one?

So, I was certain, if not one hundred percent, at least ninety-five percent, that people would not believe me if I were to tell them that the Party leader had told me that I was going to be a good orator. I thought up a scheme. There are lies that sound like truth and there are truths that sound like lies. I had to make them tell me that I was going to be an orator.

I approached my teacher; my mother and other teachers were beside her. They all congratulated me and said that they liked the speech very much. I said, "Mom, the leader told me that I would be a good curator."

They all giggled. My mother corrected me and said, "Son, he must have said orator, not curator."

I had succeeded. They were the ones who used the word orator.

My nickname became "orator" until I graduated from grade school. My mother smiled whenever my teacher called me "orator." In the end, I never became an orator. I don't even particularly like to speak in large meetings. I only became a good teacher and spoke well in front of my students.

IV

The desire for the opposite sex began to enter my body before it hit my head. The need to love someone, anyone—to be in love—was an irresistible desire. My first love, when I look back, is perhaps a laughing matter, though it certainly was not then.

I was twelve years old when I entered junior high school. Naturally, I was fifteen when I graduated, after attending the middle school for three years. Like all the children of my age, sex progressively began to preoccupy me. My hormones were raging fast and furiously. The opposite sex attracted me, but I did not know how to approach girls or exactly what to do with them. I must add that during the time I was growing up, the relationship between boys and girls was very different. Dating was not allowed; even just simple friendship between the two sexes was frowned upon. In this forbidden atmosphere, love and sex were the only thoughts at the threshold of my imagination. The best I could do was watch the girls from a distance. Today, after so many years, the situation is totally different for young people.

I had three good friends in school. Our friendship began almost from the sixth grade and continued on. Two were my age, and the third was two years older. We were inseparable during those three years, and we thought we were in love with the same girl. What follows is the story of our friendship and our first love. As I look back, I still laugh at our naivety.

I will call my friends Tom, Dick, and Harry simply because their Turkish names are tongue twisters. We studied together, we played soccer together, and during the lunch hour we munched the sandwiches we brought from home together. Yet we were very different from one another, both physically and emotionally.

Harry was very thin and tall and always looked sickly. His nose, the left nostril in particular, ran constantly. Sometimes he blew his nose into a handkerchief, but sometimes he cleaned it with the sleeve of his shirt. Each time he used the sleeve of his shirt he said very timidly, "Sorry, I forgot my handkerchief at home again." He was a generous friend. Whenever he had money, he bought chocolates, nuts, and raisins for all of us. Despite the fact that he was thin and sickly, he was the best soccer player among us. Whenever anybody bothered him he would threaten with the statement, "I'll flatten your nose right now." In fact, he really did not fight with anybody. "Never mind," he said, "I sure can flatten his nose, but then the principal would flatten mine."

I saw him carry out his threat only once. One of the bullies of the class tried to bother him by calling him "slimy Harry." At first, Harry paid no attention. But one day when we were in the garden during the break between two classes, the bully called him "slimy Harry" again, and Harry got really mad.

"Shut up," he said, "if you call me that once again I'll flatten your nose."

The bully calmly stood there and said, "Come and do it."

Harry walked slowly toward him and with lightning speed hit his nose. The bully was on the ground for a moment, but then he jumped up, grabbed Harry's neck and threw him to the ground, ready to beat him up. Tom, Dick, and I jumped on him, and before the bully could hit Harry we managed to give him a really good beating. No one touched any one of us ever again.

Tom was two years older than we were. Tall and muscular, he had flunked twice in grade school. Dick was short and fat. I was just a shade stockier than a toothpick and wore glasses. If it were one on one, the bully could have beaten the hell of Dick and me. Thank God for Tom. He really gave a good lesson to the bully. Dick and I just helped him, I guess.

I think I was Tom's best friend. We studied together and I helped him a lot. Mathematics and Turkish grammar were puzzles for him. I drilled him time and time again in those subjects and the results never went beyond mediocre at best.

Dick was very good in all subjects. He also had a wonderful sense of humor. He told us all sorts of jokes and made us laugh continuously. He was just wonderful.

What had made us the best of friends was something very unusual. Certainly it was not Dick's jokes or Harry being the best soccer player or much less Tom being our leader. As I said, all four of us were in love with the same girl. Perhaps surprisingly, this love made us best friends instead of rivals. None of us ever talked to the girl. We just used to look at her and sigh. For us she was the most beautiful girl in the world. She had jet black hair that fell on her shoulder; her large green eyes always had a sad look.

Either between classes when we had a ten-minute break or after a soccer game, we gathered together and thought about her and delved into fanciful flights. Dick fancied that he would be a brilliant officer in the army, marry her, live in Ankara, attend the balls and dance with her nonstop. Very frequently he sang a popular tango of the time, off-key, of course.

Harry described his nuptial night. She would wear a pure white silk negligee, and the bed sheets would be pure white linen. He would hold her hand and lead her to the bed. We all asked, "And then?"

Harry told us what came next. Looking back, I guess he did not have a rich imagination.

Tom was more fanciful. "Never mind," he said, "not like that. First I'll take the girl to America on our honeymoon…"

Tom went to the movies every week. He had a large allowance. The rest of us could seldom go—maybe, just maybe, once a month. Every Monday we gathered around him and he told us the latest movie he saw the day before.

"Tarzan dived into the water holding his knife between his teeth, headed straight to the alligator that was about to attack Jane, killed the alligator, carried Jane to the shore, laid her on the grass, and kissed her lips."

Or he related a cowboy movie.

"The cowboy on his horse saved the girl from the robbers, took her to his cabin, and caressed her face and hair…"

Stuff of this nature. He transposed the roles, he became Tarzan or the cowboy and told us how he kissed the girl, loved her, and how the first night was.

I had even higher hopes. "I am going to join the diplomatic corps; I will go to Europe with her; I'll kiss the hands of the ladies there…"

"Oh hush," they said, "what are you going to do the first night?"

What would I do?

"Same thing," I said, "the same thing that Tom does."

We talked about her a thousand times a day. We knew, of course, that none of these things would happen. The girl would not marry any one of us; she would not even look at us. Since we knew that, we were never jealous of each other. It was just sweet talk.

It was only a few weeks before the end of the school year and the finals were around the corner. After lunch break we again started to talk about the girl. Suddenly Tom got angry. "Enough," he said, "enough. You bunch of idiots. You think there are no other girls around here?"

We did not know what to say.

"Take out her photo from your pockets."

He was our leader. Meekly, all three of us took out the photo of Heddy Lamar, the actress whose picture was among those that were included in the bars of chocolate that our friend used to buy and the one that we adored the most.

"Tear it and throw it away."

Without a word we obeyed his command, tore the picture, and threw it away. Tom kicked the pieces with his foot.

"Come on, you bums," he said, "let's go and study, otherwise we will flunk in the exams and we will not graduate. Walk!"

We walked. I looked back for a moment. On the ground was a piece of paper and from it the green eyes of my beloved looked back at me.

For the sake of success in the exams, I had left the eyes of my first love on the dusty ground.

The house I was born in, today.

With my father one year before he died

Getting ready for circumcision.

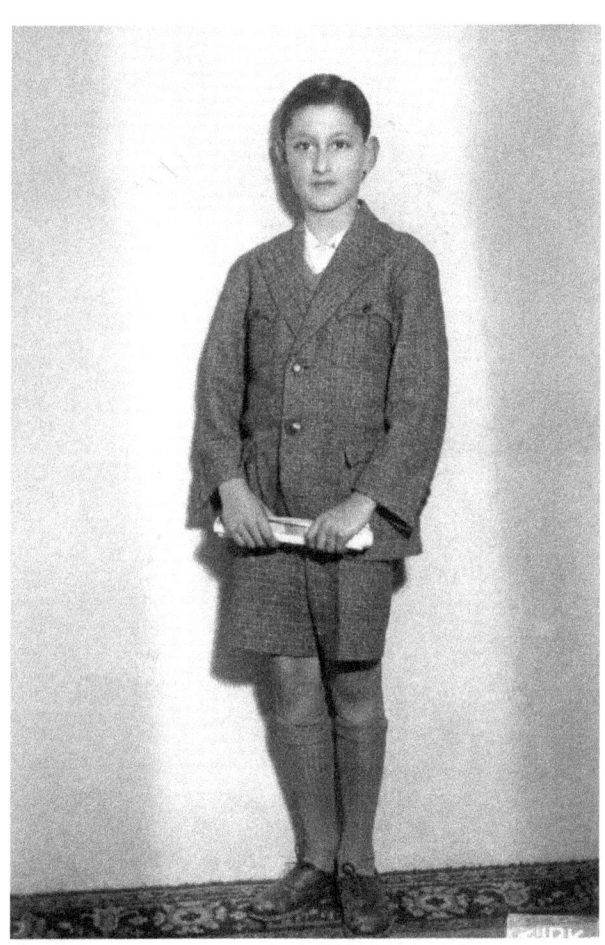

Graduation from Grade School

The year I graduated from High School

At our engagement party

In our library in San Juan

In my office at the university

In our house in Washington

5
The War Years

I

My teenage years were marred with fear of war and hardship. First the bread, and then practically everything, went bad, became adulterated, spoiled, tainted, and scarce, then disappeared from the market. Bread is the main staple in Turkey. In a Turkish household, one cannot imagine a breakfast, lunch, or dinner table without bread and plenty of it. In any city or town, bakeries are central reference points. Their windows exhibit golden brown loaves, two pounds each. From their doors emanate the warm sweet scent of baked wheat. That was always so until the Second World War began.

Turkey had signed a pact with France and Great Britain, a mutual assistance agreement, in the summer of 1939, placing the country squarely against Germany's unending appetite of conquest, and a substantial number of men had been mobilized, just in case. The wheat production plummeted, brown-crusted white flour bread loaves became adulterated with barley, corn, and millet; their size shrank, and finally they were rationed. In each neighborhood, local government offices began to distribute booklets of coupons for the daily bread. The warm, sweet scent that used to emanate from the bakeries disappeared and was replaced by an odor that was no longer appetizing.

The bread itself did not disappear from the market, but the per person daily ration was first set at half a pound, then reduced to a quarter of a pound, and later to one-eighth of a pound or two thin slices.

Two other major indispensable items for any Turk began to be scarce: tea and coffee. Tea always accompanied breakfast and afternoon snack tables. Coffee, served in small demitasse cups, was consumed incessantly. Tea from India or China and coffee from Brazil or Yemen began to disappear. Whatever was available was adulterated, tea with sage and coffee with roasted chickpeas. They had a hideous taste. The small amount of tea produced on the northeastern coast of Turkey was far from sufficient for domestic consumption; small amounts of coffee were imported irregularly. They too were rationed.

It is inconceivable for a Turk to drink tea or coffee without sugar, and yet the domestic sugar production capacity was well below the national demand. Before the war, Turkey imported sugar, but that was no longer possible. To curtail consumption, the government raised its controlled price twenty fold. Raisins and dried figs became sugar substitutes. Ersatz coffee or ersatz tea with raisins and dried figs were disgusting substitutes, indeed. As the war progressed in Europe, gloomy days followed one another in Turkey. As time went by, bread was adulterated further, and the centuries-old custom of offering a cup of coffee to a guest disappeared. Bread, coffee, tea, and all other items subject to price controls became major black market commodities at prices affordable only to the rich. Inflation was rampant while wages and salaries were frozen. Many items disappeared from the shelves of the shops. All yard goods were also rationed to the bare minimum. Misery was everywhere.

I still vividly remember queuing at the door of the local government office on the first day of the month to get the coupons for the rationed items. Either because of a paper shortage or because of the inability to organize their provision, no ration coupons were available. Instead, birth certificates were used. These certificates consisted of a small booklet that contained several blank pages, in addition to the page that registered our births, details of names of the holder, of his or her parents, date of birth, religion, city and suburb where registered. These blank pages began to be filled with stamped information that read, "for the month of − −, bread (or tea, or coffee, etc.) coupon has been issued." The ordeal of waiting for the coupons became a monthly routine.

The War Years 79

As war continued, transportation in the big cities, and most certainly in Istanbul, came to a screeching halt. This occurred, I believe, in late 1941. At that time, the main source of ground transportation in Istanbul was tramways, also called electric streetcars. Since they were of German make, they needed spare parts, and none were to be had. Those that could not be repaired were taken out of service. As a result, the number of the tramways that crisscrossed the city's streets decreased and the tramways in service became unbelievably overcrowded. People began to walk from one end of the city to another. In fact, some people preferred to do that because they did not want to be in crowded places.

As if all that hardship were not enough, there was also a typhus epidemic and hence a fear of lice. The government warned the citizens by affixing posters on walls, streetcars, and ferry boats: "LICE = TYPHUS; TYPHUS = DEATH; PROTECT YOURSELF FROM LICE." How was one going to protect oneself from lice? They are not rabid dogs that can be chased away by throwing stones at them, or wild animals that can be hunted down. This barely visible parasite traveled from one person to another, unobserved, unseen, from hair to hair, from collar to collar, in crowded streetcars, boats, classrooms, offices. One bite from an infected louse was almost sure death.

In our neighborhood, dozens of people, young and old, died of typhus fever. To undress completely every night and hunt for lice in one's clothing, in one's body, under the arms, between the legs, in one's hair became a daily routine in many households. One needed to wash with extremely hot water. This required a handful of coal and a bar of soap, which was very expensive; to take a bath had become a luxury that most people could ill afford. People flocked to public bathhouses more frequently than ever before. A feeling of doom and gloom was everywhere.

Then the rumor started that lice loved clean hair and skin. For a while, public bathhouses were almost empty. Some people came up with ludicrous remedies like mixing garlic paste with aged cheese and stuffing their pockets with this foul smelling concoction believing that lice did not like the odor emanating from garlic and aged cheese. Totally oblivious to this smell, lice traveled freely from one person to another, and the epidemic continued with its fury.

Despite the nightly examination in our house, my mother became ill. Yet we had never found a single louse on any of us. She did not die, thank God. But it was touch and go. Our house was quarantined, and no one set foot in it except the doctor. We did not visit any neighbor, and I was not allowed in school for forty days.

The war shortages had other effects as well. Istanbul is a city surrounded by the sea on three sides. Before the war, a multitude of ferries carried thousands of people from one point to another, from home to work in the morning and from work to home every evening. They didn't run as frequently now, for there was a coal shortage as well. Turkey had coal mines that produced an ample supply for domestic consumption. Now they worked at half capacity since most of the miners had been mobilized to protect the country's borders against possible German attack. City residents had to contend with a ration of a thousand pounds of coal per household in the winter. The luxury of warming several rooms in a home disappeared; a single stove barely warmed one room where families now congregated, where they cooked, ate, and slept.

The majority of the population stoically tolerated every adversity until it looked as though the Germans were ready to walk right through Turkey in order to reach the oil wells in Iraq or the Caucuses, or both. The Turkish people dreaded war, and those who remembered the Balkan War and the First World War told hair-raising stories about the brutality and horrors of those times. In order to minimize the damage of a surprise attack, the street lights were no longer used; as in London, people covered the windows of their houses and apartments with black curtains. The anxiety that these changes wrought made the nights more frightening than the days.

In 1941, the Germans attacked the Soviet Union and Turkey exhaled a huge sigh of relief. It was fairly evident that, in all likelihood, Germany was not going to attack Turkey. Though the fear subsided, the hardship and deprivation continued.

Understandably, those were not happy days for me. I entered junior high school when the war began, in September 1939; I graduated from senior high school when Germany surrendered in 1945. My teenage years were filled with so many fears—fear of war, fear of blitzkrieg, fear of being a victim of the epidemic, fear of a German occupation and all the brutality that accompanied the boots of SS officers. I was underfed, undernourished, and suffered unending colds in the winter months. Just to go to school every day became an ordeal. I would leave home while it was still dark in the morning. Down I trekked from the hills of Sultantepe to the ferry station of Üsküdar so that I could catch the ferry to cross over to the European side. Then I would walk uphill for about half an hour to reach my school. And I did the reverse when classes ended. At the end of the day I was almost always exhausted. Many an evening as I studied sitting next to the stove, I fell asleep without finishing my homework. I was tired, hungry, and exhausted.

That is one period of my life that I would like to forget. Generally, one tends to reminisce about pleasant events. I have no pleasant memories of the war years, except one. The war years made me a strong anti-Nazi, anti-fascist, pro-Jewish, and pro anyone who had seen, experienced, and hated the cruelty of the Germans. I learned to respect human life and reject any cruelty, war, or anything else incompatible with human dignity.

I must add that I know I am not as good as I describe myself. I still nurse a prejudice left over from the war years. I do not like Germans as a whole and I do not like Germany. I have been there a few times, long after the war, but I never felt at ease in that land. It is pure prejudice, I know, for I have come to know quite a few good Germans. I also know that today's Germany has nothing to do with Hitler's Germany. But I enjoy my prejudice and I am not ashamed to confess.

6
My Military Service

I

In my university years, I considered myself a socialist. The commonly accepted meaning of this word today is different from what it meant to us then. I was not only under the influence of Hegel and Marx, but had devoured the novels of French naturalists like Zola and realists like Chekhov and Gorki. My understanding of socialism contained a serious portion of humanism. To me, socialism meant the eradication of poverty, unconditional equality among citizens, abolition of the privileges of the wealthy, and no discrimination based on religion, ethnic origin, or language; it also carried the influence of the French Revolution. For me, all men were created equal. I believed in universal brotherhood, free from all prejudices.

Little did I know that I was to come face to face with the type of naked ethnic prejudice that I rejected. I repudiate that prejudice today just as I did then. Yet I was totally helpless to prevent it because of the constraints of my military rank—because I was just a second lieutenant, I had no power to reverse the decision of my captain. The motto of the Turkish army has always been, "higher rank knows better than the lower rank." What follows is the tale of an event that occurred while I was doing my military service.

As prescribed by the constitution, military service is obligatory for all Turkish men without exception, unless their incapacity is certified by a military hospital. In those days, the length of service for university graduates was one year; they served as second lieutenants. Everyone else was drafted directly into the army with the rank of private for a pre-determined period. Those who intended to study abroad had to complete their military service first.

Since I had quit my post at the university—or rather, I was forced to quit—and I had decided to obtain my doctorate abroad, I volunteered to be drafted. I was sent first to the Reserve Army Officers Training School, and with all the other inductees I was subjected to a series of tests, physical as well as psychological. These tests determined that I, and a few others, were fit to serve in the tank corps. After six weeks of basic training, we were taught all the intricacies of the death traps more commonly known as tanks. Nonetheless, we learned how to drive them, how to fire their guns, and everything else pertaining to these mobile metal canisters. At the end of six months, we all graduated and wore our officers' uniforms with a great deal of pride, the insignia of second lieutenant glittering on our shoulders. I was very proud and also very happy—actually, doubly happy. Firstly, there were rumors going around that those who were labeled leftists were usually classified as having failed the exams and then were made to serve as buck privates for two years, whether they were university graduates or not. No judge, no jury, no trial. All it took, as rumored, was a whisper from the police to the commandant of the school. I was afraid this might happen to me and was insecure until the final moment when I held my Training School diploma in my hand. Secondly, the armed forces regiment to which I was posted was headquartered just outside of Istanbul, a half-hour drive from my home. I could go to my duties in the morning and return home in the evening. It would have been a disaster for me had I been posted to some place far away at the east end of Anatolia close to the Russian border. I was lucky, I guess.

I joined my regiment in March 1952. The first morning, I arrived early at the headquarters and presented my orders to the colonel, who interviewed me briefly. I do not recall exactly what he asked me. The only thing I remember is that, since I previously had a teaching position at the university, he found me fit to serve in the Third Company and work on training the new recruits. I could not have been more content, for the desire to teach was in my blood.

The headquarters of the regiment was huge and impressive. A rectangular colossal building, it dated from the last years of the eighteenth century when it housed a newly organized army set up by the Ottoman sultan of the time. It was like a gigantic fortress that, in addition to my regiment, housed two other infantry regiments. Its inner courtyard was bigger than a football field. The story frequently repeated was that two brothers completed their military service in this same building, but never saw each other, not even once.

The aide-de-camp of the colonel accompanied me to the office of the captain of the Third Company, to whom he presented my orders. The captain was a charming but lazy man.

"Alright," he said, "go and train them. They just started their basic training. Come back to the mess hall at midday and tell me all about it. Dismissed!"

Most of the young recruits were from central and eastern Anatolia. They were all very young, perhaps twenty or twenty-one years old, but with little or no education. None of them knew how to drive a car or a truck, let alone a tank. It was going to be a tough job, but I would worry about that later. The basic training consisted of simple things like parade walking, carrying a rifle properly, and saluting. I had two drill sergeants under my command. They did the drilling and I supervised them.

That was my first day. Every day thereafter, I briefed the captain at the mess hall. He seemed to be happy with my work and inspected the company every afternoon. The progress of the company was more than satisfactory. I was quite happy and proud.

During the second week of basic training, I saw the drill sergeant beat one of the soldiers. Yes, beating was still a practice in the army then. Since I was totally against corporal punishment, I intervened at once. "Sergeant, what the devil are you doing?" was my immediate reaction.

"Sir," the sergeant replied, "this idiot does not speak Turkish!"

I looked at the face of the young soldier, a most handsome face. He had a dark complexion, and his black eyes were big with long, black eyelashes. He was small-framed and of medium height, with a very slender neck. The collar of his uniform was two sizes too big for him. He stood at attention with tears running down his cheeks. All his face muscles were contracted with anger.

"What's your name, son?" I asked him, but received no answer. "Where are you from?"

Again, I received no answer. The sergeant came to my help.

"I told you, sir, he does not speak Turkish. He speaks only Kurdish. His name is Ali."

I looked at Ali once again. The stoic expression full of anger could not hide the almost innocent baby face. It was impossible not to like him. In fact, I liked him immediately and also felt pity. A young man, barely twenty and totally lost in the maze of a language he did not understand, thrown into the army where he had not even a single friend, and now he was being beaten by a sergeant and he could not understand why. I turned to the sergeant who was standing two steps behind me.

"Do you speak Kurdish?"

"Some, sir. The village I come from is next to a Kurdish village."

With all the authority my rank bestowed upon me, I reproached him. "If you ever hit this soldier again, or any soldier for that matter, you lose your stripes. Is that clear? And tell Ali that as of tomorrow he is to come to my office after lunch every day. I will teach him Turkish."

Of course, I had no power to bust the sergeant to a private, but he didn't know that, and he was scared.

On the way home that evening I stopped at a bookstore and bought an alphabet book used in the first year of grade school. The next day Ali, as instructed, stood at the door of my office. He was unbelievably bright. In one week, he completed the alphabet book and we began reading short stories and practicing conversation. He told me about his village, a village that was remote from the rest of the civilization. He was the oldest of four boys in the family. His father had a small plot of land barely large enough to grow wheat for their own consumption. They had no electricity and no running water. It had been his job every morning to go to the stream half a mile away and return with two pails of water for their daily use. Now it was the job of his younger brother. Ali wondered how his brother was coping with it.

The cash income of the family consisted of the proceeds of wood chopped in the fall from the nearby forest and selling it in the city, which was ten miles away. He was very proud that they had recently managed to buy a donkey and his father did not have to carry the wood on his back anymore. They also had two goats, and, as he put it, his mother made the most delicious cheese, which was the envy of the whole village. He told me all this in his newly acquired language and each time he finished a sentence without any error his eyes gleamed.

I grew to love Ali like a brother. For him, I was not only his commanding officer, but also his big brother, his protector, and his only friend. More than anybody else he tried to excel at his training just to please me, I know for sure. On the rifle range he consistently hit the bull's eye. But then, I thought he must have had quite a bit of practice before he was recruited. Ali became the star of the company.

It was almost the end of basic training when an order came from Ankara. Ten soldiers from our regiment were to be transferred to another regiment located at the Russian border. Captains were to select them. Since it was not up to me to make the selection, I paid no attention to the order. A few days later the sergeant who had hit Ali came to my office.

"Sir," he said, "Ali is waiting outside and would like to see you. May he come in?"

I was a bit surprised, for Ali knew quite well that he could come to my office any time outside the drilling hours. He was my half-friend, half-student.

"Yes, of course, Sergeant, let him come in." I wondered what the problem was.

Ali entered and, as protocol required, saluted and stayed in attention. Tears ran down his cheeks.

"At ease, Ali," I said. "What is the problem? Did anybody bother you? Tell me."

Ali began to sob. "Sir," he said, "I am to be transferred, sir," and then he paid me the biggest compliment in the Turkish culture. "You are my father, you are my mother. Sir, don't let me be transferred. You will help me, won't you? Over there they will beat me again, sir. Please, sir, you are my teacher, sir. Please, sir."

The fear of the unknown, the separation from his protector and his only friend in the company, had completely panicked him. I gave him my handkerchief. "Dry your eyes right now," I ordered, no doubt a mock order. "You are a brave Turkish soldier. A soldier does not cry."

I did not know what else to say. "I promise, Ali," I said, "I'll talk to the captain."

I did talk to the captain. I told him without exaggeration what a wonderful soldier Ali was, that he was a sharpshooter, that he could take a machine gun apart and assemble it in less than fifty seconds, that he was unbelievably intelligent, and that he had learned Turkish very fast. Indeed, Ali was one of the most intelligent young men I had ever known. None of my arguments could dislodge the captain from his decision. He did not want a Kurd in his company.

I said, "Kurd or Turk, Captain, makes no difference. He is a son of this land. Please, Captain, we will lose one of the best soldiers in our company."

The captain looked into my eyes and said very curtly, "Lieutenant, a captain always knows better than a lieutenant."

The die was cast—Ali was going to be transferred. I was totally helpless.

The same afternoon another sergeant came to see me. "Sir, Ali is about to be taken to the train station. He would like to see you."

I could not face Ali. I did not have enough courage to tell him I had failed. "Tell Ali you could not find me," I ordered the sergeant.

I opted for the most cowardly route.

The sergeant who took Ali and nine other soldiers to the station told me later on that until the last moment Ali had not lost hope. He kept repeating that his lieutenant would save him from the transfer until he heard the whistle of the engine announcing the departure of the train. Only then did Ali lose all hope. He squatted in the corridor and murmured: "You are done for, Ali."

There are moments in one's life when, no matter how brave one thinks one is, cowardice takes over. Not facing Ali's situation was a cowardly act. I have always been a person who rebelled against discrimination—discrimination based on ethnicity, religion, color, creed. Yet I was feckless. I could have insisted further, but I didn't. I could have gone over the captain's head by appealing to the colonel of the regiment, but I did not. The difference in rank must have scared me; I was doubly a coward. We think we know ourselves, but there are crucial moments that show us for what we really are.

I often wondered what became of Ali. I like to think that after completing his military service, he returned to his village, married

My Military Service   89

a beautiful Kurdish girl, and had lots of children, and that he is an old man now with many grandchildren. I'd like to think that in the long winter months when his village is cut off from the rest of the world by the heavy snow that falls in eastern Anatolia nonstop, he sits in front of the fireplace with his grandchildren around him and tells them about his military service, perhaps even about his lieutenant who taught him Turkish. I would hate to think that after returning to his village, resenting the ill treatment he received in the army, he had joined the Kurdish separatist guerillas, and in one of the many mountain skirmishes that have continued on and off for many years, he was shot, killed, and that his body is in an unmarked grave.

Ali's story was a tragic experience for me. I will never forget his face, I will never forget his bright eyes. But I also had an unforgettable tragic-comic experience that added to my anti-militarist feelings. Though it might appear to be unbelievable or surrealistic, it really happened.

On a Friday morning, Ahmet, the drill sergeant, came to see me during the rest period and said there was a problem that he wished to talk about. I liked Ahmet. He was a recent graduate of the non-commissioned officer's school. He was young, barely twenty-one years old—a handsome lad from Edirne, the most westerly province of Turkey in Europe. His slight tinge of Rumeli accent pleased me, for it reminded me of my beloved aunt, my father's sister.

"Yes, Ahmet," I said, "at ease. Is there a problem?"

"Sir, I found lice among the soldiers."

Fear grabbed me. Lice! The memories of the war years were still very much alive, particularly lice and typhus fever, which nearly killed my mother.

"Ahmet, tell the captain. He must know."

Ahmet shook his head. "I dare not, sir. He will get very angry."

Indeed he would. But I had no choice; it was my duty to inform him. Not knowing what his reaction would be, I did talk to him while we were having lunch in the mess hall.

As expected, he did get angry, very angry indeed, and said, "Alright, I know what to do."

I wondered. What was he going to do? Was he going to order

the lice to march out? Or perhaps order the soldiers to catch all the lice? Our captain was a curious mixture of a Janissary and a Prussian officer. He believed that everything could be solved with an order.

As was his habit, he came to inspect the company precisely at five o'clock. But that afternoon he did not ask questions as he used to do. He did not want to know what the soldiers had learned in the training that day. He simply addressed them and said curtly, "I have been informed that there are lice among you. That is not tolerable. Tomorrow is Saturday and you will all go to the regimental bathhouse. You will wash yourselves clean. On Monday morning I will inspect all of you. If I find even a single louse on any one of you, I will put it in his palm and make him eat it."

Then he turned to me and ordered, "Lieutenant, dismiss the company!"

I was dumbfounded. As soon as I dismissed the company, Ahmet turned to me and, with two question marks in his two pupils, asked, "And now, my lieutenant, what are we to do?"

He knew full well, as I did, that making the soldiers eat the lice was not going to solve the problem.

Later on, I went to see the captain in his office and asked if he could possibly provide me with a couple of gallons of gasoline. That was all I needed.

"Why should I?" he asked.

"Sir, trust me, I shall get rid of the lice problem once and for all. If there are lice on the soldiers, there must be lice in their beds, on their mattresses, sheets, pillows, and blankets. I assure you, I will disinfect the whole company."

He looked at me with a sarcastic smile. "Well, well. Let me see what you can do. All right, you can have two gallons of gasoline. Dismissed!"

I knew exactly what there was to be done. On the way home, I bought two pounds of DDT, a deadly material that was sold in the market as pesticide. The rest was easy.

When I arrived at the barracks in the early morning hours of Saturday, my free day, I found the soldiers in their sleeping quarters, getting ready for the bath. As I entered they all stood at attention. Ahmet was there too, waiting for my orders.

"Ahmet, go and get me two gallons of gasoline from the garage. I have the captain's permission. I also want a portable pump and a hose."

What I wanted was in front of me in a jiffy. I mixed the DDT with the gasoline and ordered the soldiers to disrobe.

"All mattresses, sheets, pillows, blankets to the center of the room! And then, disrobe and put all your uniforms, underwear, socks, and boots on top of them."

First, there was hesitation as to what the lieutenant was up to. But in the army orders are orders. They had already learned to obey without understanding. The soldiers soon stood stark naked in front of me. I pressed the button of the electric portable pump and sprayed the soldiers and the material heaped on the floor.

"Now, all of you to the bath house. Quick march!"

It was a daring, perhaps even a stupid, move from my part. DDT was a toxic material and I could have caused a fatal accident. Thank God, no disaster occurred.

On Monday morning, the company passed the inspection with flying colors. The captain joked with me and after the lice incident always called me the "DDT lieutenant." Most importantly, it was the soldiers who were ever grateful to me—I had saved them from eating lice.

7
In the West

I

The year 1950 was a turning point in my personal life: I married my sweetheart and I graduated from the University of Istanbul as an outstanding student of the School of Economics. I was appointed as a teaching assistant, the very first step toward becoming a professor, after a series of hurdles and exams. I was ready to face them in due course. My aim was to be a good teacher and transmit to young minds everything I knew and was going to learn as I advanced in my professional career.

It was also a turning point in the political history of Turkey. After twenty-seven years of single-party rule, a multi-party election changed the hand that held the helm of the state. The new party that came into power under the banner of democracy was leaning strongly to the right. As a first political move, it attacked the left mercilessly. It branded the whole left—social democrats, socialists, syndicalists—indiscriminately as communists and accused them of being sympathizers of Soviet Russia, a very serious stigma as Turkey had been strongly anti-Soviet since the end of the Second World War.

A series of trials ensued, and some professors were dismissed outright and their chairs were abolished. I knew my turn was just around the corner, for I had the reputation of being leftist. I resigned from the faculty and enrolled in the obligatory military service, of which I have already written. My plan was to go to the United States after the military service, complete my doctoral studies, return to Turkey, and try my luck again at the university. No male could pursue higher education abroad without first fulfilling his obligation of military service. It was the law of the land then.

While I was in the army, my wife obtained a Fulbright scholarship and left for the United States. I had two more months to serve and I knew I could endure two months of loneliness. I had friends, and my mother was living with me. Little did I know that the cards were already stacked against me. My application for a passport was denied. I was desperate. Applications, repeated applications, protests, letters—nothing budged the passport authorities. Finally, a high school teacher of mine, the brother-in-law of an influential parliamentarian, intervened. This member of the Parliament was a good friend of the director general of security, and he arranged to meet with him. I will never know what was said in that meeting. I realized that the administration was corrupt and the influence of important people did resolve many unsolvable problems. I resolved mine as well. I was angry, disillusioned, disappointed.

One bleak and snowy late February afternoon, the director received me in Ankara in his luxurious office furnished with leather sofas and chairs, oriental carpets, and crystal chandeliers. He kept me standing for more than half an hour, and then finally agreed to issue me a passport.

His last words still ring in my ears. "Go to hell, go and do not come back. We do not need sons of bitches like you in this country."

Shocked and frozen with anger, I didn't know what to do. Was I to swallow the insult, the insult to me and to my mother, whom I loved and respected dearly? My gut reaction was to tell him that I was no bastard that he and the passport could go to hell and walk out of the office. Yet I did not follow this reaction. Perhaps I was scared, scared of what could have happened to me. So I swallowed the insult.

I left his office with insurmountable anger and began to walk toward the hotel where I was staying. I did not feel the cold or the powerful wind that was whipping around me, nor did I notice the snowflakes blowing in the air. I promised myself never to return to Turkey as long as that government stayed in power.

When I boarded the plane at the Istanbul airport to go to the United States, it had not crossed my mind that I would never permanently return to my beloved city. Instead, two opposite sets of feelings filled me throughout the trip to New York. One was joy and expectation; the other was the anger and disappointment that comes from deceit.

The hassle with the passport authorities had lengthened the separation from my wife to five very long months. She had gone to study abroad ahead of me. Five months were a very long separation from my beloved. I have been very much in love with her ever since our high school years, and, after our marriage, I was in love with her even more than I was when we met. I still am. For five months I had yearned for her warmth, her caresses and kisses, her voice and laughter. Now it was a matter of hours for us to be united and be together forever. My heart was beating faster than the revolution of the propellers of the Lockheed Constellation.

As my plane made a tour over the city after take-off, I looked through the window. The magnificent mosques and the blue Bosporus became miniatures very quickly, and soon white clouds caressed the glass of the window. "I shall return," I said to myself, "I shall return with a doctorate degree when those who tried to deny me a passport are out of power." I closed my eyes and my wife's face appeared in front of me with her blond hair and green-blue eyes. I was going to be with her soon.

Little did I know that kismet was going to knit a different web, and Istanbul was going to remain the city of nostalgia for me.

On a cloudy and cold February afternoon, I came out of Air France's Super Constellation and stepped onto American soil at Idlewild Airport. It was a long and arduous journey from Istanbul to New York. My plane made stops in Athens and Rome before it reached Paris. Immediately I transferred to the Paris-New York flight, which stopped in Lisbon, Azores, and New Foundland before it reached its final destination. All night long over the Atlantic, I listened to the roar of the four propellers and watched the red hot engines. I could hardly sleep.

Idlewild, now JFK, consisted of several individual buildings. All passengers were ushered to one of them to go through customs and immigration. The immigration officer stamped my passport, clamped a piece of paper to one of its pages, returned it to me, and said something that I did not understand. I simply smiled. To smile when one does not understand the language in which one is addressed is the only refuge.

The customs officer went through my suitcase while I waited impatiently for the formalities to end. While waiting, I put my hands into the pockets of my overcoat. For some strange reason, he got suspicious. He left his post, came to my side, and wanted to see what I had in my pockets. All he found was a pair of gloves. He said something that again I did not understand. I smiled again. He closed my suitcase. I grabbed it and left the building.

My wife, who had arrived in America five months earlier, had traveled from Ann Arbor to New York and was outside waiting for me. Because I had been accused of being a leftist, the Turkish government wouldn't allow me to travel. That long effort had caused me unending trauma. I could not be entrusted with a passport; the most basic human right was denied to me, and I felt constricted, shackled. But now I was free. Her smiling face shook off the invisible handcuffs from my wrists and I gave my wife a long kiss, perhaps the longest one I have ever given her.

We stayed at the no-longer-existent Martinique Hotel, not far from the Empire State Building, for five dollars a day. That same night, I walked through Broadway holding my wife's hand as tightly as I could. The irrational fear of losing her must have been with me somehow. The noise of the cars, the lights in the shop windows, the multitude of people walking on the sidewalks… So, this was New York, this was the United States. A different land, a different language that I did not understand but was determined to learn as quickly as possible.

The next day we flew to Ann Arbor, and the following day I started my English training at the English Language Institute. Early in the morning, my wife took me to the building where it was located, repeated again and again how to get back after the class to our small, rented quarters, which consisted of a room with a sofa bed, sink, cooking facilities, and a refrigerator. The point of reference was a movie house on State Street called the State Theater.

"Pass the movie house, go two blocks, turn left on East Ann Street to number 420," she repeated. She knew quite well that my sense of direction was very poor.

When the four-hour English class was over and the Rackham tower clock chimed one o'clock, I left the building through the door I thought I had entered and walked toward home. I walked quite a bit, but the movie house was nowhere to be seen. When the tower clock chimed half past one, I knew I was lost. Little did I know then that the buildings in America had more than one door. I had come out from a door from which I had not entered. I was in a slight state of panic, for I had no idea how to ask directions in English. I just stood there in an unknown land and tried to find somebody who spoke French. Several students passed by, but none spoke French.

After several tries, a young girl finally answered my question, "Oui."

She spoke French.

I sighed with relief. I asked her, "Où est le State Cinéma?" but I got no answer.

She shook her head. Cinema was an unknown word for her. Out of desperation, I made a circle with my thumb and index finger and put it in front of my eye. With my right hand I cranked an imaginary handle of a movie camera and sang "nanana, nanana."

She laughed. "Oh, State Theater."

Out of kindness, she changed her direction and walked with me all the way to the entrance of the movie house. All Americans cannot be bad, I thought.

I had come to the United States full of prejudices. The constant bombardment of the leftist press had painted the United States as a country of monsters and gangsters, of lynchings and arrogant people. Many of us believed it. We had the predisposition for it. Yes, a degree from an American university was a valuable asset in Turkey, but there was no reason why I should like America. In fact, I kept searching for reasons why I should not. I was to find out later on that many of them were petty or simply misjudgments, but I did not know it then.

Conformity appeared to be the main characteristic. All girls were wearing bobby socks and white and brown saddle shoes. "Disgusting," I said. On Saturday evenings, boys and girls lined in front of the dormitories and hugged and kissed each other. "Immoral," I said. Not counting the university crowd, Ann Arbor was a small city with a small-town mentality. At that time, Ann Arbor was equal to the United States in my mind, therefore Americans were a narrow-minded, uneducated lot—an uncivilized lot, I thought.

What shook my frame of mind about America and impacted me very early on was the United States Senate's Un-American Activities Committee. That was the heyday of Senator McCarthy. I viewed that as fascism, and fascism I hated. I still do.

My English had improved rapidly and I had started my graduate studies in the Department of Economics. I followed the Senate hearings avidly, not only because I was interested, but perhaps to fortify my prejudices. The hearings fascinated many of my classmates, too. When in one of the hearings a lawyer asked McCarthy, "Senator, have you no decency?" I thought it was the end of the lawyer. How wrong I was! It was the end of McCarthy. In my mind, the first light sparkled, the first question arose. In Turkey in a similar situation, the lawyer would probably have ended up in jail for insulting a legislator. Why not in America? Wherein lay the difference?

As time went by, my doubts regarding my previous thoughts began to accumulate, and with them my curiosity mounted. I decided to take an elective course on the American Constitution. I knew nothing about the American Revolution. It was not a subject history classes covered in Turkey. The year 1776 was just a date, whereas the French Revolution was the beginning of liberty, equality, and fraternity. I had read half a dozen books in French and in Turkish on the subject.

Well, at the end of the course on the American Constitution, I realized that liberty and equality had started with the American Revolution, not the French. Being an armchair revolutionary, my sympathy shifted from the French Revolution to the American Revolution. A country with its Constitution and Bill of Rights could not be all that bad.

Prejudices cannot be eliminated in one go. Time is the primordial factor in change. With time, those ideas or attitudes that are obvious but contradictory to pre-conceived notions, and therefore ignored, begin to make their dent. Prejudices are emotional and usually devoid of rational thinking; nevertheless, the brain, in its unsolvable mystery, begins to knock them down one by one. At least that was so in my case. What I wanted for Turkey and what

I thought a socialist order would bring to my country turned out to be myths that I believed in for years. Free enterprise, individual entrepreneurship, and a just legal system had created unbelievable prosperity and a far superior way of life in America. Could this be possible in Turkey? As doubts mounted, my dogmatic prejudices began to wane one by one.

I am not quite sure when I liberated myself from all my prejudices. The path of learning new ideas and revising old ones is not smooth. The human mind is not a machine; it is not a computer. It is a dynamic force that follows a process of its own. When it realizes that some stored knowledge is contradictory to realities observed, it discards the old in its own time, at its own pace.

Dwight McDonald's book, *Memoirs of a Revolutionist*, which I read in the late fifties, had quite an impact on me. I do not remember why I purchased it—probably because its title attracted me. The details of the book have faded from my memory, but I do remember McDonald's lucid arguments about why he believed in socialism and revolution in his early ages and why he changed his mind later on. His narration was impressive, his arguments were solid.

Because of that book, I began to question my own beliefs, perhaps not very seriously at first. But then other events and books had a series of cumulative effects on me. In 1956, the Soviet tanks mercilessly crushed the humanistic socialism experiment in Hungary and shot Hungarian writer George Lucacs, one of my favorite literary critics. At first, like the rest of the left, I thought that the intervention was justified, since there could be no cracks in the socialist front. But then came the Czech uprising of the mid-sixties, which forced me to review my position drastically.

I am not sure exactly when I reached the conclusion that socialism was not the solution for Turkey, or for any other country for that matter. What I originally saw in Fidel Castro was, in reality, an illusion. What I saw in the Cuban missile crisis was a cool-headed statesman on the one hand, and a bully, a coward, on the other.

There are two books in my library that I cherish and have read several times. One is *The Cancer Ward* and the other is *Gulag Archipelago*, both by Solzhenitsyn. In *The Cancer Ward*, the protagonist is a cancer patient who is sent somewhere in Central Asia for treatment. I thought the book very allegorical: the cancer patient represented the Soviet Socialist Republic with its inhumane system, alienation, and bureaucracy. At the end, as the patient is cured and leaves the hospital for the first time, he sits in a café having a cup of tea. Suddenly he notices a tree full of blossoms. He becomes oblivious to his surroundings and sees nothing but the tree. He is mesmerized. When I finished the book I, too, was mesmerized. The tree was the future, a country without socialism.

Gulag Archipelago, with its interminable details, shook me terribly. When Solzhenitsyn passed the judgment that "socialism prevents the living body of a nation from breathing," I could not help but pass my judgment also: socialism prevents the living brain from thinking.

The Soviet atrocities, the gulags, and the sacrifice of millions in the name of socialism simply became unacceptable to me. The misery of Eastern Europe, again in the name of socialism, was not something I could square with my belief in humanism and in a free society. It was in the early seventies that I was in Romania, the Romania of Ceauşescu. There, the last vestige of my belief that perhaps some kind of socialism was a panacea for development evaporated completely. I was free of my prejudices.

The hostage crisis in Iran determined my political orientation. As I became more and more familiar with American history, statesmen like Jefferson, Lincoln, and Roosevelt became my heroes. Perhaps the word hero is not quite correct, for I do not really have heroes, never had presidents I admired; perhaps to name them my "favorite" presidents would be more correct. President Roosevelt and his nation were towers of strength during the Second World War. I sympathized with the Democrats until President Carter. This nice, honest, sweet, humble man, who would have been an excellent social worker, as Churchill said of British Prime Minister Attlee, became president. The fiasco in Iran and Carter's "mea culpa" attitude brought me close to Reagan. I became an American citizen in 1971, and shortly after the presidency of Reagan, I became a card-carrying member of the Republican Party.

Not all of my intellectual change from a socialist to a believer of the capitalist system took place in the continental United States. After our graduate studies, my wife and I became professors at the

State University of Puerto Rico. Puerto Rico had been a part of the United States since the 1898 Spanish-American War. A different culture, a different language, but for all intent and purposes the United States.

I moved up quite quickly at the university. On several occasions, I became one of the advisors to the island's governors. These are really incidental phases in my life. What is not incidental is that I, as an immigrant, could move up without encountering any prejudice. I cannot say that the United States or Puerto Rico is totally free of prejudices, but prejudice is much less prevalent here than anywhere else I have been. As luck would have it, I lived in Great Britain and Switzerland for a while. I have seen many developing countries and worked in them, but I could not live permanently in any one of them. And, very much to my dismay, I cannot live in Turkey any more, either. On some emotional level, I am bound to be a Turk, because of its language, its history, its poetry and music. Rationally, I believe in individual freedom, liberty of expression, free enterprise, and capitalism. As I said earlier, this dualism does not bother me in the slightest.

II

Our graduate studies were over and we were looking for jobs, teaching jobs. No other type of employment was in our minds; our interest was in teaching. In those days it was practically impossible for a couple to obtain a position at the same university. We filed our curriculums vitae with the Placement Office of the University of Michigan, but did not receive satisfactory responses. I had an offer from a college in Oregon and my wife from an institution in Texas. We had to turn them down, for we were not going to be separated ever again. The five months she spent in the United States while I was stuck in Turkey was more than enough.

As luck would have it, two deans from the University of Puerto Rico had come to Ann Arbor in search of economists to fill two vacancies in its western campus. They had seen our curriculums vitae, found them to their liking, and called us to their hotel for an interview. My wife and I thought that the interviews went rather well. They promised that they would contact us shortly, yet two months passed without a response. Understandably, we sank into despair. Our visas were going to expire soon; if they did, we would have to return to Turkey. Both of us were reluctant to do so, for the same political party was still at the helm of the government; the security director general who had practically kicked me out of the country was still there. I was adamant about not returning to my native country as long as those bandits—as I called them—were still in power.

One day we received an envelope in the mail. On its left upper corner, the sender's address read: "Office of the Chancellor, University of Puerto Rico." I did not open the envelope, I tore it apart. There were two letters in the envelope, one addressed to me and the other to my wife, informing us that we were appointed as assistant professors and that the university was taking the responsibility of initiating the proceedings of changing our visas from student to exchange visitor, a status that allowed us to remain and work in the United States for three years.

The gloomy air of our tiny apartment turned into one of celebration. Not only did we not have to return home, but we were also rich. The salary offered was $4,200 per year. Two times $4,200 made $8,400—a small fortune. Or so we thought. From the university library, I checked out all the books I could find about Puerto Rico. I had plenty of time to read them until our departure for the island in August.

Puerto Rico, a small Caribbean island, was, according to tourist books, a paradise. The more serious books referred to it as an island with a bundle of social and economic problems. Administered as a U.S. possession by appointed governors until the early fifties, it became Estado Libre Asociado in 1952, a commonwealth in English, with an administration headed by elected governors. Spanish was the language of the island.

The Pan American flight took us from New York to San Juan, a seven-hour trip in those days, in a Constellation. We left Idlewild at midnight. I could not sleep a wink. In my mind, I kept reviewing my resolutions over and over again. First, I was going to learn Spanish as fast as I could. Second, I was going to be a teacher like Fritz Neumark, whom we adored at the University of Istanbul. Neumark was one of the refugee professors who had escaped from Nazi Germany and was offered a teaching position at the University of Istanbul. He loved his students; he respected his students and taught them everything he knew. He was kind and attentive. He treated them with a certain degree of formality, a formality but full of warmth. I was going to be just like him. Third, I was going to do lots of research and publish. Both my wife and I knew that in academia, "publish or perish" was the norm. I mentally reiterated all these resolutions over and over again until we landed at the San Juan airport. It was a warm day and the sun was rising behind the mountain El Yunque.

We were assigned to teach introduction to economics twelve hours a week. While we taught the students what we had learned at the University of Michigan, Puerto Rico also taught us economics, for it was a laboratory for anyone who was interested in economic development.

Long a Spanish colony from the days of Columbus until 1898, the island had suffered from neglect simply because there was no gold. It began to change under the American administration, but not much. The interest President Roosevelt had taken in the island was interrupted by the Second World War. It was in 1952 that conditions began to change drastically with the first elected governor. Luis Muñoz Marin, a socialist and leftist in New York in his youth, had come to the helm of the government. He was not a socialist anymore, rather very much a Rooseveltian New Dealer.

When we set foot on the soil of Puerto Rico that summer of 1956, the development of the island was in full swing. What I had studied about economic development at the University of Michigan was in application. Tax exemption to attract foreign investment, infrastructure building for growth, expansion of trade schools, strengthening of university education for capacity building—all were taking place in front of our eyes. Not only a paradise as vacationers would have it, but also a paradise for a development economist. During the second year of our stay, my wife and I co-authored our first article and published it in a prestigious European journal. We were on the road to establishing ourselves as development economists, we thought, but we also knew we had a long way to go. However, the first step was the most important.

Years passed rather quickly. We published some more research works, books, and articles. The university was impressed with our contributions, succeeded in changing our exchange visitor visas to the immigrant status, gave us tenure, and promoted us to the positions of professor. We stayed with the University of Puerto Rico until our retirement in 1983.

We had quite a number of very good students. Some of them also became professors in their own right as well as our beloved, life-long friends. I cannot judge whether we became as good as Fritz Neumark—at least we tried. Puerto Rico became our home. I became an advisor to a number of governors who succeeded Luis Muñoz Marin. We were also sought as consultants by several private enterprises.

I left Puerto Rico some years later for Washington, D.C., because a consulting firm made me an offer I could not refuse. Our home now is Washington, but also Puerto Rico. There was no way we could tear ourselves from the island permanently. Our apartment there, which we had acquired many years back, is our winter home. When the leaves disappear from the trees and the first snow is on the ground in Washington, D.C., I am excited, as I was on my first flight to San Juan half a century ago, to return to our apartment by the beach, admire the island's beauty with its blue-green sea, swaying palm trees, and to be with my long-time friends, talking to them in Spanish, the language that I came to learn and love.

III

My long years in Puerto Rico and my affinity with Ibero-Latin American culture cannot be fully related unless I relate the tremendous influence an older Spanish colleague, a refugee from the Franco regime, had on me. It is because of our friendship that I fully understood the difference between an exile and a refugee. Because of him, I appreciated and became even more conscious of what my grandparents had faced when they agonizingly escaped from their native land and were forced to take refuge in a city that was unknown to them. What follows could have been my story, but it is his.

In my early days at the University of Puerto Rico as a young professor of economics, I had a twelve-hour-a-week teaching load. My time was divided between preparing my lectures and learning Spanish, and I enjoyed them both immensely. Since I had classes both in the morning and the afternoon, I ate lunch at the Faculty

Club. I believe it was a month after my arrival and as usual I had gone to the Faculty Club for lunch. Little did I know that on that particular day I was going to meet a colleague destined to make a profound and unforgettable impact on me.

The morning sessions were over and it was noon. Two hours to kill before the next class. I really liked the club. Beautifully built right at the center of the campus, it exhibited all the characteristics of tropical architecture: an extended roof covering the porch on all four sides, supported by mahogany pillars, and rattan furniture scattered all around. Orchid plants, whose flowers were richer in color than those of the rainbow, hung from the ceiling. The surrounding garden was filled with purple, red, and yellow bougainvilleas; lovebirds perched on the branches of the palm trees that swayed in the breeze. During the lunch hour, there was always a sumptuous buffet consisting mainly of Puerto Rican food and tropical fruits: mangos, pineapples, papayas, bananas, oranges. I filled my plate, sat in a corner away from the crowd, and began to review my notes for the next lecture.

In a far corner of the club, several professors were drinking beer and discussing something rather heatedly. Being a new staff member, I did not know who they were. From their accents I surmised that some of them were from Spain. I knew that at the University of Puerto Rico there were several Spanish professors who had escaped from Fascist Spain and taken refuge on the island. Most of them were international authorities in their respective fields: cellist Pablo Casals taught at the conservatory; Juan Ramon Jimenez, a Nobel laureate, was in the Department of Spanish Language and Literature; sociologist Francisco Ayala, whose books were standard textbooks throughout Latin American universities; Gabriel Franco, who was the last finance minister of the republican government; Manuel Garcia-Pelayo, an authority on medieval political theory and constitutional law; Tomas Rodriguez-Bachiller, who had once collaborated with Einstein at Princeton University; lawyers, doctors, engineers, political scientists. They all had escaped from the Franco regime. At that time, the best Spanish university was in Puerto Rico.

While munching my meal and reviewing my notes for the next class, I suddenly heard a voice, "Why are you sitting alone? Come and join us."

It was Gabriel Franco, my colleague in the department of economics. He was signaling the group at the far end of the dining room. My Spanish was not good enough yet to mingle with the erudite members of the university.

"I don't know," I said hesitatingly. "You know, my Spanish is still so-so. I hate to make mistakes in a crowd."

Gabriel was not going to accept my flimsy excuse. "Don't be silly," he said with a smile. "The best way to improve your Spanish is to talk. So you may commit some mistakes, so what? Come. In any case, I want you to meet a very good friend of mine, Alfredo Matilla. You will like him. He is a great guy."

That is how I met Don Alfredo.

It was one of those quick friendships. I liked him immediately, and I daresay Don Alfredo liked me too. Each time we met at the club, he spoke to me about Madrid, the city where he was born and lived until the start of the Civil War. Everybody always called him Don Alfredo. Other professors were called by either their first names or simply "professor so and so," except Alfredo Matilla. The title of "don," expressing a high degree of esteem, was reserved for him, for Pablo Casals, and for Tomas Rodriguez-Bachiller. Of course, like everybody else, I called him Don Alfredo.

Don Alfredo had been an established professor of political science at the University of Madrid and had authored several authoritative books before the Civil War began. He had joined the government forces composed of republicans, liberals, socialists, communists, and anarchists. It was a war to the death, for the fascists were unforgiving. He quickly moved up in the ranks and toward the end of the war he was a major commanding one of the international brigades composed of mostly French volunteers who had rushed to Spain to save the republic.

After three years of fierce fighting, the last bastions, Madrid and Barcelona, fell into the hands of Franco's army and the republicans lost the war. A black cloud descended upon Spain. The proclamation of Franco condemned all Spaniards who had served in the international brigades to death. Those who escaped from Franco's death sentence left for new, unfamiliar countries and cultures. Refuge and exile were the destiny of many republicans. It was farewell Madrid, farewell Spain, for combatants like Don Alfredo.

After our first meeting, I sought the company of Don Alfredo whenever I had the time and opportunity. We always talked about the Civil War. The focus of our conversation was always the war and Madrid. His love for his native city was beyond description. With his broad Madrileño accent and his delightful narrative talent, he took me to every corner, every nook, and every street of Madrid. His tone was nostalgic, and yet realistic. I listened to him attentively and with a great deal of empathy. I, too, was away from my beloved, extraordinarily beautiful city, the city that I loved dearly. In those days, I used to dream that I had returned to Istanbul. Waking up was always painful and distressing. Talking about Istanbul gave me a great deal of satisfaction, almost a cathartic yet masochistic pleasure.

As my Spanish improved, I talked to Don Alfredo about Istanbul, about the Bosporus, the Golden Horn, my university, Galata Tower, the Jewish quarters of Balat, the Blue Mosque, the Old Palace, Leander's Tower, the used book sellers, the covered bazaar, and a thousand more corners of my native city. Don Alfredo became an expert on Istanbul and I on Madrid, without ever being there. Talking about our native cities was solace for both of us. Don Alfredo could not go to Spain; I did not want to go back to Turkey. Circumstances were different, but the reason was the same.

One day at the club as we were again talking about our native cities, I said, "You know, Don Alfredo, we are in the same boat – neither of us can return to our beloved cities."

Don Alfredo smiled and shook his head. "No, my young friend," he said. "Yes, we are in a boat, but the boats are very different. Yours has an anchor, mine does not. You left your native land because you wanted to do so. I know, as you told me, you left Turkey and your university because you were harassed for your political belief. You are hurt and disappointed. But, all the same, you decided to drop your anchor in this beautiful island, in this wonderful university, at least for a while, as your own choice. But my boat has no anchor. I left it at the shores of Barcelona. I am drifting, slowly perhaps, but I am drifting. I am fully aware that we are treated here fairly and with respect. But, in the final analysis, you are an immigrant and I am a refugee. The difference is enormous."

He stopped for a moment, took a cigarette from his pocket, lit it and inhaled deeply and continued. "Every separation contains a grain of madness. Mine was imposed, yours was your own choice. Don't misunderstand me—I am not saying you are mad; in fact, there is some beauty in madness at times. One does not have to be rational always, nor pragmatic. Feelings, honor, self-respect in what one believes is a grain of madness. You chose to be mad and I congratulate you.

"But I was forced to be mad. That is different. To be a refugee and an exile is a terrible experience, bitter and painful. It is denial of one's self. It is a discontinuous state of being, negation of identity. Exile is maximum alienation. One is like a toddler whose security blanket is lost forever. The streets one knows, the corners one turns every day, the door of one's home, the key one takes out from one's pocket and fits into the familiar keyhole without looking, the echoes of the voices of one's wife and children in the rooms and corridors, the aroma of the evening meal coming from the kitchen, the neighborhood butcher, baker, and wine seller who smilingly inquire about the health of one's wife and children, the faint musty smell of the books in one's office, the noise in the lecture halls—all of these are the threads of the security blanket. They are gone forever, and with them all habits; everything is gone. One is alienated from everything one knows, everything one is accustomed to. For you, my young friend, there always will be a homecoming when you choose it. For me there is none. None at least, as long as Franco is alive."

He stopped for a while and lit another cigarette from the butt of the cigarette that he had just finished. Whenever he wanted to change the subject, he talked to me about Spanish literature and Spanish music. He was as erudite in these subjects as he was in political science. He talked about Cervantes, Machado, Garcia-Lorca, De Falla, and Albeniz with great knowledge.

"Tell me," he said, "one day you told me you were translating Garcia-Lorca's poems into Turkish. How is it going?"

I started to talk about the intricacies of the images of the poet and the difficulties of finding the right words for them in Turkish. I adored his poems, but to translate them was no easy task.

Don Alfredo listened patiently to me for a while, and then said almost with a voice of protest and anger, "He was the best of his generation, and the damned fascists dragged him out into or through the streets of Granada, tortured him and killed him. He was just thirty-six years old."

The conversation turned once again to the Civil War. His stories about the Civil War were unbelievably vivid. Sometimes he repeated himself. But that was always welcomed, for he added new details, new comments, sometimes humorous, sometimes sarcastic. Most of the time when he finished his narrative, he would say, "The day that Franco goes to hell, I go to Madrid."

He often repeated one particular joke he was very fond of: "A man regularly buys all the daily papers from one of the stalls in Madrid, looks at the first page, curses, and says 'it is not here,' and throws the papers away. Day after day he repeats the same, 'damn, it is not here.' One day the vendor finally asks as to what he was looking for. The man nonchalantly answers 'an obituary.' 'But, señor, obituaries are on the last page' says the vendor. With a sad smile, the man says, 'the one I am looking for will be on the first page.' So that is it. I cannot set foot on Spanish soil until the obituary I am looking for appears on the first page of all the papers."

And after telling the joke he laughed somewhat bitterly. Eventually his joke became our in-joke. Whenever we saw each other in the halls of the university or at the club, we simply said at the same time, "not today, either."

Don Alfredo talked about almost everything related to the Spanish Civil War, except the fall of Barcelona. But I wanted to hear about the fall of Barcelona, the last bastion of the republic. I knew that Don Alfredo stayed there until the last moment. For quite some time I did not dare ask about Barcelona; in fact, I hardly asked any questions. It was Don Alfredo himself who was eager to talk, and I was an eager listener.

Several years after our first encounter, I finally gathered enough courage to ask him about Barcelona, for I really wanted to know how the republic gasped its last breath. Who else but Don Alfredo could relate the last episode of the disappearance of the republic and the Popular Front?

"Barcelona," he said.

Suddenly a shadow fell across his face and he remained silent for a while. His eyes looked at me, but I was not sure if he was actually seeing me. What had I done wrong? What had happened in Barcelona? I tried to apologize flimsily.

"Sorry, Don Alfredo," said I, "did I ask an improper question? Sorry."

His answer was slow in coming. "No, you did not," he said. "No, not at all. But of all the Spanish Civil War episodes, Barcelona is the only one I have tried to forget. I have, but in vain." He paused for a little while and kept looking at me. "All right, my young colleague, I'll tell you." He frequently addressed me as his young colleague. Many of my young friends at the university used to call me, lovingly, El Turco, but not Don Alfredo, for I was considerably younger than he was. His friendship was genuine but a bit formal.

"Barcelona," he said and again paused for a moment. His eyes were half closed.

"The war was lost. The Fascists surrounded Madrid, and there was no hope of helping the republicans there. The rest of the country had fallen into the hands of Franco. And we were retreating fast toward Barcelona for a last-ditch effort. Perhaps just to defend our honor, for there was nothing else left to defend. My international brigade, a brigade composed mostly of French, but also some English and Americans and a handful of Spaniards, had given a good account of itself in several battles, but you cannot win a war with one brigade alone. Some of us were communists, some socialists, and some simply anti-fascists. We all knew that the war was over and that everything was lost. All the same, we ran to Barcelona for the last stand."

Don Alfredo stopped for a while. Obviously, to remember the last stand of his brigade was very painful for him.

"And then," he said, "and then the disaster struck. In September of 1938, the government declared that the international brigades would be disbanded and foreigners would be repatriated to their respective countries. Prime Minister Juan Negrín announced that decision in a meeting at the League of Nations in Geneva. That was first-rate stupidity. The Popular Front fell apart. Negrín had already lost the support of the communists, and by his announcement of disbanding the brigades, he also lost the support of the socialists and syndicalists. He was hoping to de-internationalize the Spanish Civil War by sending foreign volunteers away. It was much too late. Germany and Italy simply ignored him and continued to support Franco with arms, planes, and so-called volunteers, who were in fact regular troops. We were doomed. The port of Barcelona was the only port of exit. All the other ports in the east and in the west of the peninsula were lost.

"But Barcelona was not really a functioning port any more. The fascist Italian air force, which was attached to Franco's army, subjected it to a merciless two-day bombing in March, 1938. It was in ruins. With a great deal of difficulty we managed to send most of our comrades-in-arms to France by boat. Also, the different factions of the Popular Front were fighting among themselves. The communists hated the socialists, the syndicalists hated the communists, and the anarchists hated everybody. The fight was not about how to fight Franco's army, but which faction was going to have supremacy. This was a real fight, with guns and bullets—a fratricide par excellence. Our army was disintegrating in front of our eyes. Ideological schism brought our doomsday even faster than Franco had hoped for.

"September 22, 1938, was a rainy Mediterranean day, a day of rain and tears. The brigade I commanded no longer existed. Foreign volunteers had gone home and the Spaniards in my brigade were no longer under my authority but that of their political commissars. I was temporarily assigned to a forward battalion, a battalion in name only. Nothing but a bunch of demoralized, angry young men. My job was to liaise with the government and keep the government informed about the deployment of our forces facing the enemy and the intelligence gathered about the enemy's advances. Our forces? That was a cruel joke. We were resolved to fight to the bitter end, and the end was near.

"After a lull during Christmas and New Year, the rebel army was onto us. On January 24, they were only three miles away from the center of the city. I tried to communicate with the prime minister's office with a miserable field phone. Hours passed; the deafening noises of the field guns and machine guns drew nearer and I was unsuccessful in reaching the government from my advanced post. I cranked the phone incessantly, but in vain. After several hours of trying, I was finally informed that the government had fled to Gerona. Nobody was in charge in Barcelona. It was total chaos. We had become like a blind knight swinging his sword in futility. The government had left us to the mercy of Franco, and of mercy Franco had none.

"It was then that I had an anxiety attack for the first time in my life. I knew that all my comrades would be butchered like sheep. Three years of fire and blood, attacks and counterattacks, murderous machine guns, hand to hand combats, bayonets all around me; the endless bickering of communists, socialists, anarchists in the government, in the army—none of those things ever made me lose my cool, my judgment. But to serve a government that ran away from Barcelona, that...that pushed me into a bottomless abyss. That I can never forget."

He stopped for a moment and he almost murmured, "I've read somewhere that someone once said, 'time is a purgatory that cleanses all fury from memories.' Not for me my friend, not for..."

Don Alfredo could not finish his sentence. He reached for his coffee, which already was cold. He took one sip, leaned back and took a deep breath and almost whispered, "And Barcelona fell on January 26."

His hands were trembling and his eyes were moist.

Finally, on November 20, 1975, it became the news on the front page of all the papers. Francisco Franco returned his soul to his maker. For the émigré professors he returned it to the devil. His reign of forty years built on blood and fire was over. Spain was free of Franco.

Don Alfredo was the happiest person on the face of the earth. Since his departure from Barcelona in a dingy boat to the unknown, he had lived with the desire of returning to Spain, when Franco was gone. For forty years he had hoped and prayed for this day. Finally his beloved Spain was without Franco and he was no longer a refugee or an exile.

The very same night, he hastily packed his suitcase. A couple of shirts, undershirts, a pair of shoes, socks, and a suit quickly found their way into his suitcase. With his old overcoat on his arm, one he had never worn since leaving Barcelona, Don Alfredo left his home for the San Juan airport. All his life, he had never missed a single class. The students were sacred to him. He loved all of them, he respected all of them, and the semester was still going on. But that day was not like every other day. For the first time in his life, he was going to miss his classes.

I said goodbye to him at the airport.

"I'll be coming back shortly," he said, "within one week or at most ten days. I will call you as soon as I get to Madrid. It will be a short trip this time. I cannot leave my students just like that. I have to finish the semester then I will dredge my anchor from the shores of Barcelona."

I knew what Don Alfredo meant.

I waited at the airport until the departure time and kept wondering how he was going to cope with a long night flight. He tried to be cool and calm, but I could sense that he was nervous and agitated. I kept repeating to myself, "Have a good trip, Don Alfredo, have a good trip."

But I guess it was not meant to be. It is not too difficult to imagine how he passed the hours until Madrid, but what follows is a fair conjecture.

Iberia airline's plane left the airport at six o'clock sharp. Next stop Madrid, flying time ten hours and ten minutes. For Don Alfredo, ten hours and ten minutes were longer than ten days—an unending ten hours and ten minutes. How would he pass the time? He tried to sleep, but couldn't. He looked at his watch every ten seconds. The stubborn watch showed the same time whenever he looked at it. He wanted to push the time; he wanted to push the plane. He caught himself pushing the back of the seat in front of him and felt ashamed of his moment of irrationality. He closed his eyes again and listened to the pounding of his heart. Slowly he dozed off.

He was in Madrid. He was walking slowly uphill on Gran Via. The street was full of lights. The shop windows on both sides of the avenue were as rich and beautiful as he remembered. He continued to walk. Suddenly the windows were full of broken glass and bricks that had fallen off the walls and tiles from the roofs. It was just like the days when German planes, sent by Hitler to aid Franco, bombed his beloved city.

He stopped and looked up. There was no plane in the sky. Then he looked around. Gran Via was deserted. There was no one and nothing on the street—not a single soul, not a single car, not a single sound. It was pitch dark and the streetlights were off. He was all alone on Gran Via.

Suddenly he heard the rapid fire of a machine gun and a wailing noise. In the front of the airplane cabin, a baby was crying. It had only been a dream. He passed his hand over his forehead. It was wet. He had perspired profusely. In order to wipe his sweat, he put his hand in the left side pocket of his trousers and reached for his linen handkerchief. It was not there. For all his adult life, he had kept a white linen handkerchief in the left pocket of his trousers. For the first time in his life, he had forgotten to take one before leaving his house.

He lifted his left arm and wiped the sweat from his forehead with the sleeve of his shirt. As he did so, his eye caught the time on his watch: seven more hours to reach Madrid, seven hours and an unending night. His heartbeat kept increasing, sweating did not stop, and his whole body was shaking, hot and cold flashes chasing each other. He was having an anxiety attack. "Oh my God, oh no," he kept saying. He remembered vividly the anxiety attack he had in Barcelona when the cowardly government fled to Gerona. He closed his eyes and kept repeating to himself, "no anxiety, no anxiety, no, no, no, never again." He pressed his hands on his heart, took deep breaths one after another, and closed his eyes.

He found himself in Plaza Mayor in old Madrid. He walked until he came to the center of the square. Then he saw the sign for the Tavern of Luis Candelas. He used to frequent this tavern, named after a very famous bandit, with his friends. It was there that every Friday night, after his lectures at the university, he met his friends and the conversations, discussions and, more often than not, animated arguments followed bottles of wine, and the bottles of wine followed the animated arguments. For old time's sake, he wanted to enter the tavern and have a glass of red wine. He turned the doorknob and pushed. The door did not open. He pushed again and again; the door was firmly locked. Disappointed, he turned to the right and went down a few steps and found himself in the avenue. Just a little farther was the restaurant that had been at the same location since time immemorial, his favorite restaurant Sobrino de Botín.

He almost ran to the restaurant and kept repeating to himself, "I hope it is not closed, oh God, I hope it is not closed, don't let it be closed." The beat of his throbbing heart was just as loud as his footsteps. The restaurant was open. He entered and looked around. Nothing had changed. The red and white checkered tablecloths, leather-covered chairs, legs of smoked pork, sausages, and empty wine bottles hanging from the low ceiling of the bar area. All were there, except the customers. The room that was always full in the old days was now totally empty.

The emptiness did not vex him, and for a split second he was vexed that he was not vexed. There was one single waiter standing at the far corner. Don Alfredo sat down on the nearest chair and ordered roast pork and a bottle of red wine. The white-haired, unbelievably old and incredibly thin waiter with a face resembling a skull looked at him without moving. He only smiled pitifully.

Don Alfredo repeated his order, almost shouting: "roast pork and a bottle of red wine." The waiter approached him, but instead of walking, he just glided over and touched Don Alfredo's shoulder with his cadaverous hand.

Don Alfredo jumped and opened his eyes. The seat belt almost cut his stomach. It was the steward. "We have an hour and a half to land in Madrid. Would you like some breakfast?"

He looked blankly at the steward for a moment and shook his head. He could not swallow a thing, not even his own saliva. He pressed his hand on his heart. One hour and a half, one hour and fifteen minutes, one hour, half an hour, the screech of the tires touching the tarmac, engines roaring with reversed thrust, brakes, and parking. Madrid.

I received no news from Don Alfredo for a week. I was somewhat apprehensive, for I was expecting a phone call as he had promised. Nothing. And then came the sinister news, the black news. Don Alfredo was dead. I had lost my best friend; I had lost my mentor. The one who taught me not only the political and the military history of the Civil War, but also Spanish literature, Spanish music, and the beauty and intricacy of the Spanish language. I felt all alone in the halls of the university.

A week after the news, I finally gathered enough courage to visit Don Alfredo's widow to offer my condolences. It was the most painful task I had ever endured. She received me most graciously.

I kissed her hand, mumbled and stammered a few barely intelligible words to express my deep sorrow. She acknowledged them by a simple bow of her head.

Sitting in Don Alfredo's study, an embarrassing silence ensued. Finally, I managed to ask her with a trembling voice as to what really had happened. She remained silent for a while, obviously trying to compose herself and gather enough strength to narrate the last moments of Don Alfredo. Her voice was very sad, but serene and uninflected.

"As the manager of Barajas airport informed me, based on the statements of the eyewitnesses," she said, "Alfredo was one of the first to descend from the stairs to the tarmac. And as he had promised himself year after year, day after day, he knelt down, put his head on the tarmac, and kissed the soil of Madrid. The rest came very quickly."

She paused for a moment.

"The airport ambulance stopped in front of the man kneeling with his head on the tarmac. Two paramedics jumped out of the ambulance and placed my husband on a stretcher. One of the paramedics put the stethoscope on his heart and listened for a minute or so. While removing the stethoscope from his ears, he turned to the other paramedic, closed his eyes, shook his head, crossed himself, and murmured: 'In nominee patris et filium et espiritus santis...' And my husband was no more."

The silence in the room was dense and heavy, except for the occasional clicks of the rosary beads in her hand. A horrendous thought crossed my mind. Could this also be my last moment? Was I going to die one day without ever seeing Istanbul again? I still remember the instantaneous shivering in my body. I shook my head violently to dispel such a thought. I just wanted to say a few consolatory words to her, yet I was unable to utter even a sound. Something in my throat had tightened.

8
From Professor to Consultant

I

Yearning for a totally free life, free from university politics, classroom obligations, and faculty meetings, I took early retirement from the university where I had taught more than twenty years. I wanted to read and write and do research at my own pace, complementing it with sporadic consulting. I had been involved in consulting, but only in Puerto Rico. I had worked as fiscal adviser to three different governors of the island and could now complement it with assignments abroad. False modesty aside, I was rather well known in my field.

My first consulting job abroad was with an international organization. One assignment led to another, and soon I had more offers than I was willing to accept. I valued my leisure, but I was also enjoying what I was doing, for it gave me the opportunity to travel frequently, to visit a great number of countries, but, perhaps most importantly, to help those who sought my assistance.

It did not take me long to realize that consultancy combined many pleasant and satisfying aspects. True, to a certain extent it was mercenary work—its income supplemented my retirement pay. I did not always go wherever I was requested, for I was somewhat picky in the choice of the countries. But I did go to those countries where living conditions were rather dismal. At first, many were designated "underdeveloped countries." Subsequently, the label was changed to "developing countries," not that the labeling made any difference. However, some were indeed developing, and it gave me pleasure that I could contribute, albeit a grain, to improvements in them.

Consulting is like missionary work, too—in a sense, it is a weird combination of technical and missionary work. Thoreau once said, "If a man has committed some heinous sins and partially repents, what does he do? He sets about reforming the world." I did not commit heinous sins, but certainly I did set myself to reform, if not the world, some countries at least. And that requires a certain degree of empathy with the country in which one works.

A consultant needs to understand the people with whom he works. His greatest remuneration is not so much the monetary compensation, but the spark of light he sees in the eyes of those to whom he transmits technical knowledge. That remuneration is no different from the one I received as a teacher when I saw sparks in the eyes of my students. Even a single spark was worth far more than my monthly salary. That was what I felt then and what I still feel now when I work as a consultant.

Thus, I was part teacher, part missionary, and part mercenary. The standard joke in my new profession was that "a consultant is the one who will tell you the time if you will lend him your watch." I take great pride that I never borrowed anybody's watch. I told the time, always, as I knew it. Sometimes they believed me, sometimes they did not. But that is the fate of consultancy.

As a consultant I have taught, but I have also learned. The first important lesson is that consultants can help reform countries if countries themselves want to reform; consultants can help if they are asked to. Knowledge cannot be transferred if the reception is not there. Perhaps the greatest, but far from the only, challenge of consultancy is to create receptivity, not by order, not by imposition, but by conviction. Secondly, I also learned that there is a precondition to creating receptivity, and that is to change the mindset in these countries.

Most of the time, the reference point of the people is their own country, their own mores, habits, and customs. To change, let alone modify, this reference point is the most difficult challenge. One of my experiences will illuminate this. Another is a tragic one beyond description. It is the story of some emigrant families, emigrants to their homeland, who were faced with an indescribable misery and despair. Being a descendant of emigrant families myself, I am compelled to tell their story, for as a consultant, I believe I was able, to some extent, to alleviate their abominable conditions.

II

"You speak Turkish, don't you?" my driver asked in a thick Azerbaijani accent. He was taking me around in Tbilisi, Georgia, for some sightseeing. I had been there for almost a week as an adviser to a United Nations Workshop in 1984, teaching African technicians how to formulate industrial policies. I must admit, I was treated royally, though royalty was banned in the Russian vocabulary of the time. I was given a car, a driver, and an interpreter; I was lodged in a luxury hotel, though the definition of luxury is open to interpretation. My colleagues were allocated just one minibus.

I was rather curious as to the reason why I was treated differently. I was accompanying two director generals and two section chiefs, all of whom had diplomatic passports, and I was an adviser to the mission with an ordinary American passport. Little did I know that in the Soviet ranking lexicon, the title of adviser was higher than director general. I must confess I made no effort to correct this translation error.

My interpreter was a young Russian, a member of the Party. He spoke in English with me and in Georgian with the driver. He was a university graduate and very proud of his attire. The suit he was wearing had been purchased in Helsinki and his tie in Paris. He said he traveled abroad quite frequently. I got the message: he was a trusted member of the Party and perhaps a KGB agent as well. My conversation with him therefore was quite measured.

Gorbachev was firmly in the saddle and words like glasnost and perestroika were entering into everyday vocabulary; "wait and see" was in the air; the cold war was beginning to wane. No confrontation seemed necessary, though I never hid my contempt for the regime. By that time, my sympathy for a socialist system had turned to disgust; whatever measure of sympathy I once had was far behind me after the horrendous experiences I had in Romania in 1974, where the system had turned decent human beings into robots.

My interpreter was quite polite and soft-spoken, yet did not disguise his contempt for the United States. On several occasions, he tried to cajole me into polemics, but I successfully warded off any openings. Before we left Vienna, we were nearly brainwashed with the instructions that we were not to enter into political discussions with anybody, irrespective of circumstances.

He appeared to be fully briefed. He knew a lot about me, that I lived in the United States, but was born and raised in Turkey. In his eyes, however, I was an American and he wanted no direct confrontation. He accompanied me wherever I went. He fetched me from my hotel in the morning, with the car and driver, of course, took me to the conference hall, and at the end of the meetings brought me back to my hotel. He was my interpreter in the shops and restaurants. The only place I could go alone was my hotel room. Only the guests were allowed into the rooms, no one else, thank God.

The hotel had a weird system that I learned was the rule in every Soviet hotel. As I registered I was given an identity card; showing this card to the elevator operator allowed me to take the elevator to my floor, where I would give it to the floor attendant who duly noted my arrival time in a book and gave me the room key. When I left my room, the procedure was reversed. As much as I disliked this control, I sometimes went to my room merely to free myself from the interpreter. Quite a few times he wanted to have a drink with me at the hotel and I always refused, politely, of course, because he really bored me.

The driver was a young man in his early thirties. His worn-out jeans, his cap, and his unshaven face never changed. He always smiled and nodded his head when I bid him good morning and goodbye in Russian; that effort exhausted fifty percent of my vocabulary in that language.

On one particular day, my driver came alone. Presumably the young interpreter had called in sick and another interpreter could not be found on the spot. Things did not work in a hurry over there. "Liberty at last," I thought to myself, and indicated to the driver to take me a bit around the town before dropping me off at the conference hall, and I also communicated that I wanted to take some pictures. International sign language works everywhere. He nodded with a smile, which that day was bigger than usual. I wondered why for a moment and then found out.

I had no idea that he knew Turkish, for he never spoke to me while the interpreter was around. With the best Azeri accent I could imitate, I told him of course I spoke Turkish. How come he spoke it? He said he was born of Greek parents; he was neither Georgian nor Azerbaijani, but had spent some time in Baku. He was quite fluent in Azeri, but mixed it with Russian and Georgian. It was not always easy to understand him.

The gist of his life story was that he was married, had three children, one boy and two girls, was working as a driver for the government (who else?) and lived in a one-bedroom apartment in a high rise. He earned the equivalent of some thirty dollars a month and paid eight dollars for rent, utilities included. "Isn't life wonderful," he asked me, "wonderful in my country?" I told him it was—Tbilisi was a beautiful city, people were nice, and the shops empty.

While we struggled with my Istanbul Turkish (my fake Azeri accent was no use) and his Azeri mixed with words I did not understand, we made our way to the center of the city. My eyes caught sight of a long queue composed mostly of babushkas, with kerchiefs on their heads, carrying baskets in their hands. I asked him to slow down so that I could find out what they waited for.

"No need," he said, "onions just came to the market." He smiled and asked me, "Do you have good onions in America, really good onions?"

Now, an onion is an onion, perhaps of different colors and sweetness. I am no onion expert. I told him we had onions in the supermarkets; one could buy any quantity of onions as one wished, any time one wished, and they seemed O.K. I confessed my knowledge of onions was very limited.

He proudly announced that he knew a lot. In fact, he was raising onions on his balcony. "My wife does not have to queue for onions, you see," he said.

I concurred that that was wonderful.

For a while, our conversation stalled. I was the one who did not pose any questions, for I wanted him to open up on his own accord. He did so. He was very curious about me. Was I married? Did I have children? What was my job? Did it pay well? He was impressed by my answers.

"Why don't you move to our country?" he asked. "You are such an important man, the government may even give you a two-bedroom apartment although you have no children."

How generous! I told him thanks, but no thanks. I was very happy where I was.

"How can you be?" he asked. "America is full of gangsters and very expensive, and lynchings take place every day." Without waiting for my answer he added, "How much rent do you pay?"

I told him I paid no rent; I owned my house. He did not expect that answer. He was stumped for a minute.

"Still," he said, "you can have lots more things if you come to our country permanently. The government can give you all you want."

My answer was the same: thanks but no thanks.

He was not the type to give up easily. He embarked on proving his point. With an air of confidence he put me to a test. "Do you have a car?"

I told him I had two, one for me and one for my wife, and one of them was a Mercedes. Impressed, but not ready to give up, he fired the next question, "Do you have a television?"

Yes, I had two, one for me and my wife and one for the maid. Silence reigned in the car. I said nothing, neither did he. Suddenly he stopped the car, turned to me, and asked in one breath, "Do you have a video player?"

Videos were quite new in Soviet Russia; they were mostly contraband and very few people could afford them. I was in a bind. I did not have a video—never felt the need for one with so many cable channels. I did not watch television all that much anyhow. But if I were to tell him the truth, and even if I succeeded in explaining to him the cable network, I was doomed. Television channels, other than the one controlled by the government, were incomprehensible for him. He would never believe that I could have all the luxuries of television, cars, house, and a good salary, if I did not have a video player. If I were to tell him the truth, I was going to be a big liar in his eyes. I was going to betray the image he already formed of me in his mind as a well-to-do American. I had no choice but to lie.

"Yes, of course," I answered, "I do have a video player, for that matter many people in America have video players."

He fell silent and thought for a moment, started the car, and without looking at me and said, "Now I understand. You will not come to our country permanently...What shame, such a big man that you are...but if you have your video...no, you will not come here."

With those words, the remainder of the ride to the conference hall was made in an awkward silence, neither of us having anything more to add to the conversation.

III

I was contracted by an international organization to help the government of an African coastal nation, whose name I will refrain from mentioning, to help reform its tax system. When I arrived, my attention was first drawn to the inordinate number of beggars in the capital city, a city that was indeed one of the poorest and most miserable I had ever seen. More than half of it was sheer slums. The buildings, which looked as though they hadn't been maintained since their construction, were decaying. The so-called paved "main streets" were full of potholes, while the rest of the roads were simply plain dirt.

The beggars lining the streets were truly professional and appeared to have a system to which they scrupulously adhered. Their tactics of begging changed according to their ages. The teenagers followed one tactic tenaciously, surreptitiously citing the few Arabic prayers they had managed to memorize without really knowing what the prayers actually meant. Running away from them was no solution, for they ran even faster. Attempting to take refuge in one's car was of no avail because they would simply lie down in front of it and cry, "Help, I am hit." Miraculously, a policeman would appear on the scene from nowhere. Although he could have been of some assistance earlier, he seemed to only notice the beggars who feigned the accident. The next step was the police headquarters, which meant a bribe that was much heftier than what the teenagers had hoped to extract.

Shortly after I arrived, I was told what to do to avoid such unpleasantness: "Always keep a handful of small change in your pocket. When the urchins accost you, throw all the change you have as far as you can and run in the opposite direction."

Old beggars were mostly sedentary and maintained their work stations on the street corners. These people were blind, lame, disfigured—some with just one leg, others with one arm—and all were poised to exploit the sensibilities of the passersby to the hilt. There was no gender bias among the beggars. This was one area in which women had equal rights and opportunity. Adding to the picture of their misery were the babies they held in their arms, malnourished infants whose faces seemed to be coated with black flies. All of them were polyglots. They begged in a number of languages: English, French, Italian, even Russian. "Good morning," or "good evening," followed by "please." With their extended hands, their eyes begged, the babies cried. I cannot forget those beggars.

The city was dirty and always dusty. As people dumped their garbage onto the street, an unusual food chain began its work of reclamation and recycling. First, the poor, the homeless, and the beggars would sieve through the garbage looking for anything to salvage and whatever might be edible. Next came the street dogs to glean what they could from the trash pile. What remained was a feast for the cockroaches. While nothing was wasted, the stench that hung over the city day and night seemed to be an almost inseparable fixture of the environment. Once in a while, the wind blew from the sea and brought some badly needed fresh air.

A famous Arab traveler who had visited this land in the early fourteenth century had written: "We came to the harbor early in the evening. The stench coming from the city was so strong that we decided to wait until the next day." Obviously nothing had changed in seven centuries.

One of the newcomers to the age of colonization had incorporated this poor land into its empire late in the nineteenth century. Why this was done could only have been for the sake of glory (!). This semi-desert arid land had never had any riches to either develop or exploit. The colonial power that absorbed this poor area built a Gothic-style church, which now lay in ruins, since no Christians lived in this land. An arch of triumph had also been built in the center of a park, which the citizens used as a pissoir at night.

After the Second World War, the colonial power departed. During the years of the cold war, the leaders of the African country played the game of smiling sometimes to the West and sometimes to the Soviets. I was told that during the years of friendship with the Soviets, a team of Russian experts proposed building a slaughterhouse, for the animals were simply being killed on the streets. The consultants came, the consultants left, and finally, with Soviet assistance, a modern abattoir was built adjacent to the only beach the city had, discharging its refuse into the sea. The beach became shark-infested. When the Soviets left, the Americans came and built a base somewhere in the desert.

It was a moot question as to why the country needed fiscal reform, since it was a country where nothing really worked. Nevertheless, all international organizations were united on this issue; they insisted that fiscal reform was necessary, but never really gave any thought as to whether it was feasible. Reform means doing away with corruption, bribery, and influence peddling. The government had no intention of reforming the tax system. Their system was based on bribery and corruption. Yet missions came, missions left, reports were written, press conferences heralded the advances that would be made as they moved on the road to reform.

That experience gave me one of the best lessons in my consulting career, one that I shall never forget. As a member of a large mission, I established quite a good relationship with the director general of customs simply because I spoke French. No one else in the mission was familiar with that language, and the director general, by virtue of having a doctorate degree in economics from the University of Nice, spoke only French as a second language. Customs administration was one of the areas that the mission was keenly interested in reforming; hence, I was asked to undertake its scrutiny. I established amicable relations with the director general. Frequently, I invited him out for coffee or lunch, and I chatted with him until he developed a certain degree of confidence and trust in me.

One afternoon as we were having coffee in the garden of a hotel and talking about the reform, he said quite frankly, "Fuat, why don't you give up this reform business? If you do, you can contribute to our country beyond your imagination."

After having worked there for three weeks, my thoughts were quite similar to his; of course, I was in no position to say that, neither to him nor to my colleagues in the mission. I had no choice but to pretend that what he was saying was utterly outlandish.

"Oh no, that would lead to disastrous results. If we do not carry out the reform, you have to say goodbye to the assistance coming from international organizations. Without such help, your economy, which is already on the brink of disaster, would really sink into an abyss, God forbid."

My newly acquired friend laughed bitterly. "Look, my friend," he said, "maybe others may not understand, but you can. You also come from a developing country. You are almost one of us."

He stopped for a moment and, locking his eyes onto mine, continued. "I am a director general, right? Well, my legal salary is $35 per month, just $35. Last week, my eldest son wanted a pair of blue jeans. So we went to the market. The cheapest one was $20. You calculate the rest. Of course I take bribes—so does the minister, so does the customs inspector at the docks, so does everybody else. You tell me how I can survive without bribes if you shut the sources of additional income. I know it is not legal, I know. But how do you think we can survive otherwise?"

I had no ready answer, yet I continued to return to that nameless country. I continued to work on fiscal reform, though admittedly, without any appreciable improvement. During one of my subsequent visits, which turned out to be the last one, I learned that the previous minister of finance had lost his sinecure job and that a new minister had been appointed. The new minister, perhaps to please the international organizations or maybe, just maybe, wanting to improve his ministry, had appointed a young U.S.-trained economist as vice minister. The reform appeared to have gained some impetus and the new round of reform discussions was rather heated.

After one of the meetings with him, I was about to leave his office with my colleagues when he asked me to remain behind. I was curious to know what he had in mind. He pointed to the chair in front of his desk, bid me sit, and began to talk.

"With God's help I think we will succeed in reforming our tax system. As you see, the young generation is at the helm of the administration. But I need your help. Please don't say no to me."

I had no idea what he really wanted from me. I mumbled, "If it is something that I can do, of course."

With his finger he pointed to the wall behind me and said, "I will order that a door be opened there; the next office is yours. Just work with me for a year and advise me on the completion of the reform, O.K.?"

I was dumbfounded; I did not know what to say. Two, perhaps three weeks in that city was tolerable, but a year was a sheer impossibility. The vice minister kept on talking. He would give me a car with a chauffeur and a house furnished by the government. I could name my salary.

"It is impossible," I said, "my wife is still teaching; she cannot leave her job. And for me to be here alone…"

I could not finish my sentence. He laughed at my incomplete statement.

"I know what you are thinking," he said. "That is really very easy to remedy. We can get you a temporary wife. Look, we can go to any of the nearby villages. You look around, pick any young girl you fancy—a virgin, of course, and a beautiful one at that. A most beautiful virgin can be had for, at most, two camels. As soon as we give two camels to her father, you would have a temporary wife."

I was utterly speechless. Fiscal reform in a country where the price of a beautiful girl was simply two camels!

He hurried to add, "Don't worry, it will cost you nothing. I can buy the two camels from the budget of the ministry. Just say yes."

I did not say yes, nor did I say no. I just said, "Let me think about it. I will let you know next time I come."

There was no next time. One of the generals decided to be the president and a civil war broke out. The people who gave the impression that they were easy-going, gentle, kind, and sweet were at each other's throats. They killed one another without pity, destroying and burning the city repeatedly, and of course the reform was totally forgotten.

IV

Early in the nineties, I received a call from the United Nations. Would I be interested in designing a project to assist displaced persons in Crimea? Naturally, I accepted eagerly. Crimea as a region interested me very much. More importantly, the subject was assistance to displaced persons, and in this case the term euphemistically referred to the Tatars who were taken out of their homeland by force because of the whims of Stalin; many of them had become destitute refugees.

For centuries, Crimea was the homeland of Tatar Turks. The khanate had become part of the Ottoman land during the reign of Sultan Suleiman the Magnificent in the sixteenth century. The khan kept his throne but the peninsula remained under Ottoman suzerainty for two centuries until Tsarina Ekaterina captured it and added it to her empire at the end of the eighteenth century. During Soviet times, it was administered from Moscow as a semi-autonomous land.

In 1944, calamity fell on the people of Crimea when Stalin decided to deport all the Tatars to Central Asia en masse with the pretext that some Tatars had collaborated with the Nazis when the German army occupied Crimea for a brief period during the Second World War. Stalin was punishing all the Tatars for the collaboration by a handful. They were guilty by association, when in fact thousands of young Tatars had fallen when fighting with the Red Army against the Germans. Stalin did not believe in individual punishment, his policy was collective punishment. So, no Tatars were left in Crimea; all of them—young ones, old ones, males, females, babies still suckling their mothers' breasts—were loaded onto cattle wagons and exiled to Central Asia. They were replaced by Russian families that Stalin sent to the peninsula for settling.

Not all Tatars survived the journey in the cattle wagons—elderly ones died in the wagons and babies expired in the arms of their mothers. Only half of the half a million Tatars finally reached their destination to resettle in various cities of Soviet Central Asia. Fearful for their future, they made superhuman efforts to survive. The green hills, fertile valleys, orchards, vineyards, and the cool breezes blowing from the Black Sea with its abundant fish became bittersweet memories while trying to survive in the arid zones of their new region. To return to Crimea was an unending but hopeless desire. Even to move to more favorable parts in the region was an impossible dream. They were forbidden to travel outside the area where they were ordered to live—better still, to survive. After half a century, many who were born in Crimea died and were buried under the sandy dirt. The young ones grew up listening to the tales of El Dorado, called Crimea.

In 1989, Gorbachev lifted the ban; the Tatars could now return to Crimea if they so desired. This time it was exile in reverse. The return to the land of their forefathers was an inextinguishable desire. Yes, they could return to Simferapol, to Bahcheserai, to Yalta, to Evpatoriya, but even cattle cars, in which the exile to God-forsaken places had taken place, were not available. They were on their own. Most sold whatever meager possessions they had and bought third-class train tickets. Thus began the reverse trip. Now Crimea was the end station of the steel rails. Thousands, hundreds of thousands, flocked back to Crimea.

Total deception waited for those who returned. Their houses were taken over; they were not theirs any longer. Their land was occupied by others. The fruits of their orchards were gathered by those who were sent there by Stalin's orders. Tatars once again became destitute, disillusioned, and desperate refugees in their own homeland. The Tatars who were displaced were displaced once again, and in their own homeland.

It was the United Nations that heeded their plight and began to develop programs through UNDP (United Nations Development Programme) to help IDPs (internally displaced persons). UNDP asked me to go to Crimea and design a project to resettle the returning Tatars. It was quite a challenge, but, given my sympathetic disposition toward exiles, I did not think twice. I took the first flight to Crimea.

Crimea was no longer a part of Russia. After the demise of the Soviet Empire, it became an autonomous republic within Ukraine. I first stopped in Kiev for a briefing and then flew to Simferapol, the capital of the autonomous republic. Then I began to travel all around the peninsula just to gather my thoughts as to how and in which way I could design the project.

Crimea was more beautiful than I had imagined, and the Tatars were charming. Hardened by adverse conditions, they were determined to recapture their homeland. I collaborated perfectly with them, for, as opposed to many professional experts, I had the advantage of speaking their language. Tatar Turkish is very akin to the Turkish I speak. If not a brother, I became a cousin to them. They opened their hearts to me. They told me their aspirations, their desires, their hopes for the future. A great many of them lived in temporary shacks with no running water and electricity, waiting to be settled.

I worked day and night, and with the help of my Tatar cousins I designed a project that answered the most immediate needs of these brave people who were starting from scratch. I am proud to say that I succeeded in designing a project that UNDP accepted to implement and asked me to monitor its execution. This gave me the opportunity to return to Crimea fairly frequently. I believe Tatars turned the corner—they built roads with their bare hands and established schools for their young, all thanks to the help of UNDP.

On my third trip to Crimea, I encountered an incident which caused me great pain. I will never forget it, nor do I want to forget it. It involved the case of a woman who was first an exile in the steppes of Central Asia and then a destitute emigrant, not in a foreign land, but in her own homeland. The project was progressing very successfully; however, the deputy mayor of the city told us—a group of experts and a couple of United Nations officers—that some hundred families were still living in a temporary shelter awaiting settlement. He wanted us to visit them. Naturally, we agreed.

He took us to a building that was an old warehouse. The Tatar families were living in its cellars, consisting of windowless stone basement rooms. A cold and damp air hit our faces as we entered. Pipes that ran over the ceilings were covered with dirty green moss. Bunk beds were arranged on top of one another. Children played on the bunks. Old people with yellowish skin were lying on the bunks, the deep creases on their skins hiding a thousand sorrows.

We left the cellar in a hurry.

Totally shaken by what we had seen, all of us were mute for a long while when we were outside. We were trying to recuperate from the shock. The appearance of a middle-aged woman from the cellar broke our silence. She was wearing a dress made of the cheapest cotton cloth. On her feet she had a pair of old thongs. Her hair was whiter than her age warranted. Her blue eyes transmitted both sorrow and anger. She spoke to us in a croaky voice also full of desperation. I remember until today word by word what she told us.

"We came to our land because it is ours. I sold my wedding ring; my mother sold her wedding ring just to buy a train ticket. Now in our own land we are living like animals. I guess we must be animals, for this is the tenth time these foreigners are coming to see us like seeing the wild animal in the zoo."

She took a deep breath and turned to the deputy mayor.

"How many times will you show," she made a wide circle with her hand and repeated, "show all of us to these people like animals in a zoo? My mother is slowly dying of rheumatism. She can walk no longer; her crooked fingers cannot hold a spoon. We have been living in this place for three years, three long years. Is it our destiny to be buried alive in this dungeon? Why did we return to our homeland? To die here like rats, is this our destiny?"

I really do not know what else she said, for her words could not penetrate my ears any longer; my brain simply refused to register this unbelievable human tragedy. My face was all wet; my uncontrollable tears were running down my cheeks. What my grandmothers had told me about their ordeal suddenly felt like a pleasure trip. To be destitute, a hopeless emigrant living in such conditions in one's own land was an insurmountable sorrow.

I walked toward the nearest wheat field, for I did not want anyone to see my tears. It was the end of summer and the ears of grain were golden yellow. But they did not belong to the Tatars.

I tried to design an emergency solution for those families. I am proud to say that I was successful. Within a short time, they all were taken out of those shelters that were not fit to live even for animals and resettled in a small village. I do not know what happened to them thereafter. But they could not have been any worse. No one could.

Epilogue

Whether one is a refugee, an exile, or an immigrant, the result is always the same. Left behind are loved ones, old habits, and familiar surroundings—surroundings that are like the strongest fortress, protecting the very existence of being. Also left behind is one's language, the most precious, inner part of any human being. Nothing is dearer or closer to the soul than the words heard from birth to death. Language is more precious than the most beautiful music, sweeter than the sweetest of all songs. The mother tongue does not come from the brain, but from the soul.

A refugee is the one who escapes, an exile is the one who is forced out, and an immigrant is the one who opts for a new land, a new harbor where an anchor can be dropped. I have seen them all. My parents were children of families who left their land and moved elsewhere for self-preservation. What they left behind became unattainable forever. Their nostalgia and longing for the past never died. I have seen the exiled.

Some of my teachers at the University of Istanbul were exiled Germans. They had taken refuge in Turkey, running away from certain death at the hands of the Nazis because they were Jews, socialists, or just honest men who could not compromise their principles. But in fact, they felt they were exiles and not refugees, for they hoped that one day they would return to their homeland, to their language. Indeed, a few of them did. My Spanish colleagues at the University of Puerto Rico were also exiles, and one day they were going to return to their beloved land. Franco was not immortal.

While to take refuge elsewhere or to be exiled in a foreign land is an involuntary act, immigration is a voluntary one. No one, no power forces the immigrant to leave the homeland. It is a voluntary act at the cost of leaving behind an inextricable part of oneself. Memories linger in one's mind, memories of no importance, incidents that should be forgotten—but they are not. Memories of great significance, memories that change one's life, are carved into the depths of one's brain. An immigrant lives in two different worlds at the same time.

I witnessed this duality while I was growing up, but perhaps I failed to fully understand its meaning and its contradictions until I felt it become a part of my life. One cannot live in a new country without loving it, respecting it, and, in an egoistic sense, being happy in it. I could not be any happier than I am in the United States. It is my adopted country. I love it, I admire it, and I cannot conceive of living anywhere else. But my yearning for the old country still lingers. This yearning subsides with time but never disappears. The cells in my brain, in their own warped logic, keep bringing to the surface memories like faded photographs. They fade with time, but never disappear. My love for Istanbul never dies down. In every opportunity, I go back to my native city just to see the places that are engraved not only in my brain, but also in my heart. After one of my many visits I wrote the following lines.

> Many times we said farewell
> Many times we found each other.
> The song I want to sing to you
> Hides itself behind my tears.

www.ingramcontent.com/pod-product-compliance
Lightning Source LLC
Chambersburg PA
CBHW032052150426
43194CB00006B/500